THE JACOBIN CITY
A PORTRAIT OF NORWICH 1788–1802

THE JACOBIN CITY

*A Portrait of Norwich in its
Reaction to the French Revolution
1788–1802*

BY

C. B. JEWSON, F.S.A.

1975
BLACKIE & SON
GLASGOW AND LONDON

Published by
Blackie and Son Limited
Bishopbriggs, Glasgow G64 2NZ
5 Fitzhardinge Street, London W1H 0DL

ISBN 0 216 89874 9

Printed in Great Britain by
Robert MacLehose and Company Limited
Printers to the University of Glasgow

To

Sir Arthur South
Lord Mayor of Norwich 1956,
Leader of the City Council at
the time of its abolition

Contents

List of Plates

Introduction

This book is an attempt to describe the society of Norwich in its reaction to the French Revolution. A century earlier Norwich had been the second city in the Kingdom in population. By 1788 when this story starts it had been overtaken by Bristol and by some of the great new conurbations like Manchester and Birmingham. It still remained one of the most important manufacturing centres in the country, a fact which made the government very sensitive about revolutionary movements here. As the various cities of the realm functioned in accordance with their individual charters which had been granted at different dates to meet differing circumstances, every one had developed its own political peculiarities. Many corporations were self-perpetuating oligarchies and apart from London, Norwich was probably still the largest of those boroughs which were democratically governed. The corporation here was subject to the pressures of two recognisable party groups related to the tories and the opposition whigs in national politics and there was some sort of a balance between them. In other cities the set-up was different. In Leicester the corporation was dominated by High Church tories, the opposition of Dissenting manufacturers being barred from office by the operation of the Test Act. In Nottingham on the other hand the whig dissenters generally had the upper hand and were apparently strong enough to prevent the Test Act being invoked. Lincoln was a tory city where the mob could enjoy burning Tom Paine in effigy and no one dared raise a voice for reform.

The balance of the parties in Norwich and their ability to work together despite the violent reactions aroused by war and the Revolution lends an especial interest to the local story and may be seen as the beginning of a fruitful tradition which has developed over two centuries and in our own time has enabled

Labour to take a dominant part in local politics with a degree of conscious civic pride as great as that of the older parties.

This book covers the fifteen years from 1788, the centenary of the Glorious Revolution, to 1802 when the treaty of Amiens brought briefly the peace the whigs had long striven for. As with the Munich Agreement in our own time the peace proved ephemeral and its supporters were soon compelled to realise that there could be a price too high to pay, and so politics took a new tack.

Chapter 1 gives a general picture of the city at the time in question: chapters 2 to 8 cover its political history over the period, with a journal of civic events and some accounts of actual contacts with France and personal reactions to the Revolution: chapters 9 to 12 describe the activities in other relationships of life of some of the characters who appear in the political chapters. There is of course much more that might be written.

Considerable attention is paid to the religious dimension as it is contended that religious affiliations largely determined the political outlook of those we are concerned with and that the religious alignment in Norwich differed from that in most other cities. Here a powerful Anglican Establishment symbolised by the Cathedral and the great church of St Peter Mancroft was matched by scarcely less powerful congeries of Dissenters headed by the wealthy and highly literate body worshipping at the Octagon Chapel.

The materials used in the compilation of this book are listed in the appendices. Much reliance has been placed on the two local newspapers, the *Norfolk Chronicle* and the *Norwich Mercury* and where no other reference is given the information may generally be taken to come from this source. Of the manuscripts referred to the Kinghorn papers comprising principally a monthly exchange of letters between Joseph Kinghorn of Norwich and his father in Yorkshire from 1791 to 1799, are in the author's possession. The numerous contemporary books and pamphlets are all to be found in the Local History Library at Norwich Central Library, where the staff have given me the most ready and willing help.

1 *The City and its People*

A fine old city, truly is that, view it from whatever side
you will; but it shews best from the east where the ground
bold and elevated overlooks the fair and fertile valley in
which it stands. Gazing from those heights the eye beholds
a scene which cannot fail to awaken . . . feelings of pleasure
and admiration. At the foot of the heights flows a narrow
and deep river, with an antique bridge communicating
with a long and narrow suburb, flanked on either side by
rich meadows of the brightest green, beyond which
spreads the city: the fine old city . . . with its venerable
houses, its numerous gardens, its thrice twelve churches,
its mighty mound. . . . There is a grey old castle upon the
top of that mighty mound; and yonder rising three
hundred feet above the soil, from amongst those noble
forest trees, behold . . . that cloud-encircled cathedral
spire, around which a garrulous army of rooks and choughs
continually wheel their flight.[1]

Such was the city of Norwich as described by George
Borrow, painted by Crome and Cotman and drawn by the
Ninhams and other artists of the Norwich School.

In the 1790s the population was slightly declining and stood
just below 40,000. Of these some 2000 were scattered in the
outlying hamlets which came within the city's jurisdiction and
the rest lived in the old walled town or close outside its walls.
For this number there was plenty of room. Besides the thrice
twelve churchyards there was a good deal of garden ground.
Lord Bradford's house in Magdalen Street (later sold to the
Blind Institution) had no less than four acres. Matthew
Brettingham's garden outside St Augustine's gates was big
enough for him to set man-traps in it after being robbed of the
oak stakes supporting his espaliers. The great houses in
Surrey Street (still surviving as Norwich Union offices) had

gardens stretching back to the city wall with thorn trees and tall elms, and even fully built-up street frontages concealed surprising patches of garden behind their dwellings. There were some 7500 houses in the city. Many were of venerable age; some very large like Bacon's house in Colegate which has survived from Tudor times to the present day. An advertisement in 1795 describes another mansion house with gardens and offices in St George's Colegate. It had two drawing-rooms and a study looking south onto pleasure-grounds planted with shrubs, a handsome vestibule, ante-room, dining-parlour and butler's room. There were six bed-chambers with closets on the first floor and attics and a laundry above them. Below stairs were two kitchens, a housekeeper's room, servant's hall and larder. Besides these there were cellars, a brew-house, double coach-house and stabling for five horses. From the upper rooms could be seen views of the cathedral, river and adjacent country. The house was said to have cost £8000 and was offered on a 100 years' lease for £800 with a ground rent of £11 per annum.

The flint walls with their gatehouses which ringed the city were not well thought of. The gate on Bishop's bridge was pulled down in 1791 and the *Norfolk Chronicle* rejoiced that St Stephen's gates were to meet the same fate. In 1792 John De Carle and Philip Barnes contracted to demolish five more gates for £60. Thomas Peck writing ten years later considered that the taking down of the gates admitted a current of salubrious air and that it would be a further improvement if such parts of the walls as were not built against were also removed.

Some well-to-do citizens had moved out to houses in the hamlets around the city—James Crowe to Lakenham, Jeremiah Ives to Town Close House, built on the Freemen's pastures, Joseph Gurney to The Lodge, whose grounds are now occupied by the City College. John Gurney had moved in 1786 from Magdalen Street to Earlham. Besides these mansions within and without the walls there had been substantial building in recent years of which a good example remains in Thomas Ivory's great terrace in Surrey Street. All these houses, besides the families of their owners, sheltered numbers of servants. A modest bachelor establishment like that of Frank Sayers in the Close included two female servants, while someone came in to clean the knives and shoes and to rake and weed the garden.[2]

A large class of inhabitants were shopkeepers, living over their shops. The directories of 1783 and 1802 list over 300 shops and there were doubtless many more too small to be listed. Some, for instance the grocers, were well-to-do and no doubt supported sizeable households. Grocers who were also tallow-chandlers were required to pay £25 on being admitted freemen whereas bakers paid only £6 and cordwainers £5.

According to the *Norfolk Tour* a great many of the smaller houses in the walled city were pulled down in the latter half of the eighteenth century to make room for improvements and the people were rehoused outside the walls.[3] No doubt a large proportion of the dwellings were very small and the majority of these were inhabited by weavers for weaving dominated the city's trade and was important to the economy of the villages around Norwich also. There are said to have been some 6000 looms in the city. These were installed in the top story of the weavers' houses with wide windows to catch the maximum of daylight for their operation. A few weavers' houses which have survived may be identified by these windows. When work offered the weaver might labour for many hours together. John Pitchford, writing in *The Cabinet* in 1795 said:

> The weaver enters his loom at four in the morning and with an hour for his meals remains till ten at night. Is it not intolerable that men should thus be converted into machines and beings who possess the power of reasoning and the faculty for enjoyment compelled to labour for a bare subsistence?

Not everyone took so dim a view of the weaver's life. John Fransham a poor scholar, denied the means of learning through the death of his patron, gave up writing in an attorney's office and put himself under the instruction of a journeyman weaver, Daniel Wright. They worked in the same room but the noise of their shuttles did not preclude conversation. Fransham said that Wright was a man of fine philosophical spirit and well able to discourse on the nature and fitness of things. He preferred this occupation to "writing" and stayed at it until Wright died two years later.[4]

There were weavers who found time for other interests. Sir James Edward Smith, writing in 1804, said that cultivators of fine flowers were very numerous among journeymen weavers and others employed in the manufacture. Joseph Fox, a weaver then living, was the first person who ever raised a Lycopodium from seed.[5] Cultivation was of course not a monopoly of the weavers. Samuel Briggs, a cordwainer, who died in Doughty's Hospital in 1797 was the last survivor of a society of herbalists in the city who claimed to have been the first to propagate the rhubarb plant in England. Poor Briggs had performed on the French Horn in the Mayor's procession until superseded by a more adequate player. On being dismissed he begged—and was granted—permission to keep his usual place, promising that when he put the instrument to his lips he would not disturb the harmony of the band by blowing it.[6]

Some weavers too had serious religious interests. Joseph Kinghorn wrote in 1792:

> Our lectures are very thin indeed owing in some con-
> siderable degree to a good cause—a Quantity of Work
> which confines the attention of our labouring poor w^c.
> is a very pleasant thing for a place like Norwich that lives
> chiefly on one manufacture.

If the labouring poor attended the lectures of this learned young Hebrew scholar no doubt other ministers had a similar following.

Richard Beatniffe estimated in 1795 that the general run of weavers would earn 6s a week though the more expert might make between 14s and 21s. The weaver was seldom dependent on his own wages alone. His wife and children could earn money by spinning, pipe-filling and other operations. Beatniffe considered that an industrious man and his family could earn and live comfortably on 10s to 12s a week—a decade earlier he had put the figure at 9s to 10s. In his opinion:

> They who can earn 14s to a guinea a week too often
> spend that in idleness which can be procured with so much
> ease and work two or three days only instead of six.

Of the tradesmen auxiliary to the weaving industry, dyers and hot-pressers would earn 15s a week and combers 12s.[7] These wages depended on work being available. For unemployment there was no help except the allowances made by the Guardians of the Poor. In the case of sickness weavers—and others—helped themselves by banding together in a number of Friendly Societies. As one of these put it:

> If it please God to afflict you with lameness, sickness or blindness that hinders you from following your business, calling or occupation, you shall be relieved. . . .[8]

These Societies or Purses were usually based on a particular inn where they met to pay their subscriptions and held their annual feast. A typical society would collect 1s a month from its members and pay out to those unable to work 8s a week for the first month and lesser sums thereafter. In 1789 a brewer in whose business many Purses had invested their funds was declared bankrupt and a public subscription was raised to make good their losses. Lord Buckinghamshire was so impressed with the importance of the matter as to subscribe 100 guineas.

The provision of work was the care of the manufacturers who distributed materials to the various craftsmen and organised operations and the merchants who disposed of the finished product. About a quarter of the production went by broad-wheeled wagons to London while the rest was loaded onto wherries and barges for delivery by river to Yarmouth and ultimate export.

These merchants and manufacturers were the leading citizens of Norwich and the builders of the great houses designed by Thomas Ivory and other architect-builders. They were strongly criticised by J. W. Robberds, the biographer of William Taylor, who wrote:

> Their personal conferences in matters of business were almost exclusively with those dependant on them for their daily bread or who benefited by the operations of their trade. . . . Accustomed to have all their commands implicitly obeyed, they too often became proud, severe, impatient, authoratative, overbearing and dictatorial.

B

Reverenced as patrons, they acquired the influence of
Lords.[9]

Robberds had no doubt particular people in mind but as a
generalisation his criticism can scarcely be justified for the
active part taken by the merchants and manufacturers in the
democratic politics of the city argues an ability to cooperate
rather than dictate.

The city's streets at this time left much to be desired. Many
were paved with cobbles as Elm Hill is today. A visitor who
generally took a favourable view of the city wrote in 1792:

> The streets—they cannot well be said
> To merit praise; they're badly laid,
> Crooked, unequal and uneven,
> And rugged as the path to heaven.[10]

Besides this catalogue of defects many of the streets were
woefully narrow. In October 1790 the shop window of Mr
O'Brien, hairdresser, in London Lane was demolished by a
wagon-load of hay pressing against it. The *Norfolk Chronicle*
lamented that the greatest thoroughfare in the city was scarcely
wide enough to allow such a body to pass. Traffic was a
constant cause of trouble. Victims of accidents were frequently
admitted to the Norfolk and Norwich Hospital. In 1795 the
authorities were urged to bring to justice young men who
endangered life by driving market-carts furiously along The
Walk and up and down Gaol Hill. Horses would sometimes
get out of hand. One day in May 1791 the porter of the Lynn
wagon was thrown by his horse in St Giles' Street. The horse
then ran full speed down Guildhall Hill and fell on the pavement by the window of Mr Oxley's hat shop. Recovering its
legs it ran down The Walk, knocking down an old man and
oversetting his barrow of oranges, steered its course between a
ladder and a wagon at Mr Back's, proceeded up Hog Hill (now
Orford Hill) and forced its way into the kitchen at the Post
Office where it was secured. Sometimes citizens used the
highway for dumping refuse. In 1796 someone was fined for
leaving rubbish in St Augustine's Street, which nearly caused
John Harvey's curricle with Mrs Harvey and two children
aboard to be overturned.

Of the public open spaces the Market Place was most important. It was the venue for large political meetings and the site of the polling booths for both city and county elections. It was the centre for public celebrations, bonfires, parades and civic pageantry. Its common use was graphically described by the Rev. Joshua Larwood, a country rector, writing in 1800.

> The market-place, which is nearly an oblong square, and a very fine one, lies upon a slope with exactly sufficient inclination to shew to advantage the successive rows of peds (semi-circular hampers) as you view them from the bottom. The market women are ranged in equidistant rows, with a regularity little short of military precision; between these rectilinear divisions sufficient space is preserved to admit the concourse of buyers. . . .
>
> At the bottom is another space of parade-like appearance, emphatically called the Gentleman's Walk: this walk on the market-day is thronged with a collection of very interesting characters; the merchant, the manufacturer, the magistrate, the provincial yeoman, the militia officer, the affluent landlord, the thrifty and thriving tenant, the independant farmer, the recruiting officer, the clergy, faculty, barristers and all the various characters of polished and professional society.[11]

The marketing habits of the time were described by Dr James Martineau. It was, he wrote, the duty of every materfamilias to sally forth on market days before breakfast to lay in the needful stores for the larder. His mother used to take him to help with porterage. They went pretty early but were almost sure to meet Mrs John Taylor on her return from market bravely struggling with her load. She would never pass them without stopping for a chat, often running into grave and stirring themes. His boyish sense of humour was touched by the effect of so much eloquence from the lips of the old lady, weighted by her huge basket, with the shank of a leg of mutton thrust out to betray its contents.[12]

There were other public open spaces—Chapel Field, which was not much used by the genteel because of the number of disorderly boys congregating there, especially on Sundays—

and the area round the Castle, thus referred to by the writer of
A Norfolk Tale (1792):

>   ... a terrace falls
> With gentle slope from those dread walls
> Where beauty holds its daily court
> And all the Norwich belles resort.

Important too in the social life of the city were the Pleasure
Gardens, particularly Keymer's Vauxhall Gardens with their
octagonal Pantheon between St Faith's Lane and the river and
Quantrell's (later Coe's, then Neech's) Ranelagh Gardens
outside St Stephen's gates. Here concerts, fireworks and other
entertainments were organised in Assize weeks, on Guild day
and on other suitable occasions. The charge for admission to
the gardens was usually 1s with 6d returned in free liquor.

At the northwest corner of the marketplace stood—as it still
does—the Hall in the Market or Guildhall, the centre of civic
government. Lower down near the river was the New Hall, or
St Andrew's Hall, the great church of the Blackfriars, which
the city had acquired when the friary was dissolved and which
was used for such meetings as could not be accommodated in
the Guildhall and for the Mayor's annual banquet. The
numbers of carriages bringing guests to the banquet posed a
considerable traffic problem which was solved by instituting a
one-way system. Carriages were required to approach the Hall
from the Duke's Palace and to leave by St Peter Hungate.
Cross traffic was prevented by stretching a chain across the
north end of St George's Bridge St.

Norwich was well provided with inns, the principal being
The Angel and The King's Head in the market-place, The
White Swan in St Peter's and The Maid's Head (still extant) in
St Simon's. Besides providing refreshment, accommodation
and club-rooms, these inns played a vital part in the elaborate
and comprehensive transport system. The Expedition Coach
for the summer season of 1790 left the King's Head at 3pm,
travelled via Newmarket and reached London at five next
morning, the fare being 21s inside and 10s 6d outside. The
Daily Coach from the Swan was cheaper, 16s and 8s. Prices
fluctuated but tended to go up over the years, in 1795 they

were 31s 6d and 16s, in 1802 42s and 22s. Wagons set out twice a week from the Star in the Market place for York, while some 120 carrier's carts travelled once or twice weekly from forty different inns, calling at practically every village in Norfolk. The river also provided a means of transport. Wherries sailed from Norwich to villages on the broadland rivers. Regular barges left for Yarmouth on Mondays and Thursdays returning on Tuesdays and Fridays. These connected with London and Hull coasters or the packet boat to Cux-haven which sailed from Yarmouth twice a week. Besides all this the river provided the city—as it still does—with drinking water and its upper reaches were a favourite bathing place. In 1789 Mark Wilks, the enterprising Baptist minister who farmed land at Heigham, set up a bath house on the river there, naming it Fort George and advertising it as fit for the reception of the Prince of Wales.

The city's inns, important as they were, were not always of good repute. In 1791 a subscription was raised to buy up an inn in Lady's Lane with a view to pulling it down and so removing a "nursery of vice and debauchery" which was an annoyance to visitors to the near-by theatre.

The Theatre, modelled on Drury Lane, and the neighbouring Assembly House had been built by the enterprise of the notable architect and builder, Thomas Ivory, earlier in the century. The latter was the centre for the social life of the well-to-do, the scene of balls in Assize week and at other times. It happily survives and has been restored to public use through the munificence of the late H. J. Sexton.

To the thrice twelve medieval churches had been added a number of meeting houses of dissenters. The religious affiliations which divided the citizens into various denominations had originated in the turbulent days of the Tudors and Stuarts. In the reign of Elizabeth the fierce protestantism of the citizens had been reinforced by an influx of refugees from the Low Countries. In the time of Charles I there had been a strong reaction against the High Church views of Archbishop Laud as enforced by Bishop Wren. After the Revolution settlement of 1688 there remained an important minority of religious dissenters. The Presbyterians included a substantial body of well-to-do citizens who wished to be free from episcopal control and in practice were not subject to presbyterian discipline either. In 1756 they had built the Octagon of which John Wesley wrote in the following year:

> I was shewn Dr Taylor's new meeting house, perhaps the most elegant in Europe. . . . The inside is finished in the highest taste and is as clean as any nobleman's saloon. The communion table is fine mahogany; the very latches of the pew doors are polished brass. How can it be that the old coarse gospel should find admission here?[13]

Wesley's last remark was no doubt a dig at Dr Taylor's tendency to unitarian doctrine, but the unitarianism of the Octagon did not prevent the common use of the term Presbyterian to describe its congregation nor discourage adherents of other denominations, including occasionally Anglican clergy, from attending there to enjoy the eloquence of the highly cultured ministers who served its pulpit. The Independants, descendants of those who had gone to Holland to escape from Bishop Wren's brand of churchmanship and had there developed a Congregational polity, had built a splendid baroque meeting house which after the Octagon was built close by came to be known as the Old Meeting by contrast. They had stiffly maintained the calvinistic doctrine inherited from the sixteenth century reformers. In this they were followed by the Baptists who had their meeting house in St Mary's, who shared a common origin with them. The Quakers, originally break-away extremists from the Baptists and Independants, were the most uncompromising of dissenters, and had a meeting house in Goat Lane near the fashionable quarter of St Giles'. They had built another of magnificent proportions in the Gildencroft, Over-the-Water. For the Methodist preachers the Countess of Huntingdon maintained the Tabernacle just outside the Bishop's garden, while the Roman Catholics had a chapel in St John's Maddermarket, now converted to the Maddermarket Theatre, and another in St Swithin's.

The ancient churches whose towers punctuated the townscape were the preserve of the Anglicans except for the small St Mary the Less which housed the remnants of the French congregation. Many were spacious buildings in the perpendicular style of architecture, the most important and most magnificent being St Peter Mancroft, across the market place from the Guildhall, whose peal of bells was rung on all joyous occasions. Standing up above the church towers the city was dominated by the ruinous but solid cube of the Castle Keep—still serving as a prison—and the slender spire of the cathedral rising from the low ground by the river.

REFERENCES

1. George Borrow, *Lavengro*.
2. W. Taylor, *Collective works of the late Dr. Sayers*, p. lxxix.
3. R. Beatniffe, *Norfolk Tour.* 5th edn 1795, p. 73.
4. W. Saint, *Memoirs of the late John Fransham*, p. 79.
5. J. E. Smith, *Biographical Memoirs of several Norwich Botanists*.
6. *Norwich Mercury*, 7 Jan. 1797.
7. Richard Beatniffe, op. cit., p. 76.
8. Rules of a Friendly Society of all trades at Queen Anne Alehouse, St Michael's Coslany. NRO.
9. J. W. Robberds, *Memoir of the late William Taylor*, vol. I, p. 40.
10. *A Norfolk Tale*, 1792.
11. J. Larwood, *Erratics*, p. 112.
12. Janet Ross, *Three Generations of Englishwomen*, p. 20.
13. *Wesley's Journal*, vol. III, p. 315.

2 The Revolution Society

The year was 1788. William Pitt had been in power as Prime Minister for five years. The American colonies were lost and Pitt had been engaged in reconstituting the finances of the country and restoring its prestige. In 1785 he had proposed a mild measure of Parliamentary Reform but his own followers would have none of it. He had secured the peace by concluding in 1787 a Treaty of Commerce with France, enabling the subjects of both countries to reside and travel in either without licence or passport. This year Pitt's friend, William Wilberforce had brought in his first Bill to abolish the slave trade but the Bill had fallen before the opposition of the Liverpool merchants and the general indifference.

In Norwich on 5 November the city guns were fired and St Peter's bells pealed. The Mayor and Corporation went in procession to the cathedral. There was a bonfire in the market place and the houses round were illuminated while a band played patriotic tunes. All this was to celebrate the centenary of the Glorious Revolution of 1688 when James II was thwarted in his attempt to impose absolute rule on the country. The settlement then made by Parliament with William III had ensured that the House of Commons was henceforth dominant in English affairs. The revolution had been "glorious" in that no blood had been spilled either in the field or on the scaffold and that by it the old blood-feud of Roundhead and Cavalier, of Anglican and Puritan, was stanched. But as the purpose of the exercise had been to confirm the existing law against a law-breaking king one of the effects of the revolution was to strengthen the existing centres of power and privilege and to entrench them against reform. On the occasion of the centenary, the *Norfolk Chronicle* wrote (1 November 1788):

> The Revolution is undoubtly the most illustrious and happy aera in the British annals. . . . Hence Britain has

been . . . the grand bulwark of the liberties of Europe and of the Protestant religion. Hence agriculture, manufactures and commerce have risen to a height which has surprisingly increased the wealth of the community. Hence science, polite literature and the arts of social life have been improved in a manner that . . . cannot be equalled in any part of universal history.

That evening 102 gentlemen dined at the Maid's Head Inn with John Barnard, a dissenter and leader of the reforming party, in the chair. A score and more toasts were drunk. "The immortal memory of King William" called forth three cheers. "The Bishop of the Diocese" was toasted as were "The Lord Lieutenant" and "The City Members". There were more radical toasts too: "The Majesty of the People", "Equal liberty to all mankind and virtue to defend it" and "Freedom to slaves". Besides all this the diners made a handsome collection for the prisoners in the city gaols.

Not long after this celebration events in France began to give a new content to the word revolution. The *Norwich Mercury* in a despatch dated from Paris on 28 December wrote that the idea of liberty, in fact of English liberty, was prevailing there to such a degree that it was easy to forsee the constitution of France as nearly resembling that of England as the different circumstances of the two nations would admit.

A section of the community with a special interest in the centenary of the revolution was the dissenters. Their forebears had been among its chief beneficiaries. The Toleration Act of 1689 had suspended enactments denying them freedom of worship and had established their churches as a legitimate form of religious observance. They made up the backbone of the Blue and White (reforming) party. The Presbyterians at the Octagon chapel provided much of the intellectual leadership; the Quakers with their meeting in Goat Lane were dominated by the Gurney clan; the Independants at the Old Meeting and the Baptists in St Mary's and St Pauls were influential among the shopkeeping class. Now a move was afoot to obtain political as well as religious freedom by the repeal of the Test and Corporation Acts which hampered their participation in public

affairs. William Windham, MP for the city, presided at a
meeting of the Independant Club held at the Angel in April
1789 when Sir Thomas Beevor proposed a toast to "the liberal-
minded Members of Parliament who voted for the repeal of the
Test and Corporation Acts". He then went on to propose
another toast which aroused even more enthusiasm: "The
friends of freedom all over the world and success to the third
estate of France in their noble struggle for liberty".

The Norwich newspapers carried weekly accounts of the
developments in France and there were Norwich citizens who
could and did go and see for themselves. One at least was in
Paris at a very critical time and has left an account of what he
saw—Dr Edward Rigby. Rigby was a prominent citizen. A
grandson of Dr John Taylor, for whom the Octagon chapel
was built, he was born in Lancashire in 1747 and in due time
sent to Norwich to study medicine. Here he remained for the
rest of his life becoming eminent in his profession and a leader
in civic affairs. In 1788 the city fathers bestowed on him the
honorary freedom of the city in recognition of his services in
reorganising the catering arrangements at the city's workhouses. Now in July 1789 he travelled with three friends to
Paris. Finding that the Palais Royal was the centre of political
information they took rooms at an hotel near by. They attended
a session of the National Assembly at Versailles and were
caught up in the enthusiasm of the hour. Rigby wrote:

> I have been witness to the most extraordinary revolution
> that perhaps ever took place in human society. A great and
> wise people struggled for freedom and the rights of
> humanity; their courage, prudence and perseverance have
> been rewarded by success and an event which will con-
> tribute to the happiness and prosperity of millions of their
> posterity has taken place with very little loss of blood and
> with but a few days interruption to the business of the
> place.

On the afternoon of 14 July, returning from a visit to the
Monçeaux gardens, Rigby's party learned of the attack on the
Bastille and saw a crowd proceeding towards the Palais Royal
with acclamations of joy. When it came near enough they read

on a paper carried on a pole, "La Bastille est prise et les ports sont ouverts". The news was greeted with shouts and shrieks, leaping and embracing, laughter and tears. Some of the crowd recognising them as English embraced them—"For Frenchmen", said they, "are now free as well as yourselves; henceforward no longer enemies, we are brothers and war shall never more divide us." This joyful crowd was followed by another of a different character. As the English pressed towards it they saw two bloody heads—those of the Governor and the Major Commandant of the Bastille—carried on pikes. Shocked and disgusted they made their way back to their hotel.

Next day they tried to leave the city but after being twice hauled back amid the jeers and insults of the crowd they decided to wait till the commotions subsided. On 17 July they secured a place on a balcony in the Palais Royal from which they witnessed the return of the King from Versailles. He travelled, Rigby noted, in a large, plain coach with eight horses and received neither applause nor insult. The procession included the whole body of the États Généraux—the Noblesse, many of them tall elegant young men with large white feathers in their hats; the Clergy, some dressed in lawn with pink scarves and gold crosses; and the Tiers États, for whom the enthusiasm of the crowds was reserved, clothed like inferior gownsmen of an English university. That night illuminations honoured the King as Restorer of French Liberty and Father of his People. Next day Rigby's party watched the battlements of the Bastille tumble and the morning after were able to leave the city without molestation, their enthusiasm for the revolution unimpaired.[1]

Before Rigby's account reached home, the fall of the Bastille had been reported in the Norwich papers. On 3 August Joseph Kinghorn, minister of St Mary's Baptist church, wrote:

> I rejoice in my very heart at the destruction of that most infamous place, the Bastille, which the populace are regularly demolishing without any interruption from government who evidently dare not meddle with them.[2]

This seems to have been the majority view. The *Norwich*

Mercury, in an article published on 11 July, brushed all doubts aside:

> The apprehensions of some of certain bad consequences to be feared if the French should become a free people, are too ridiculous to be seriously answered.

Eleven months after the event, the fall of the Bastille was still considered of topical interest. When William Quantrell advertised the Guild Day entertainments at his Rural Gardens in June 1790, he announced:

> The evening's amusements to conclude with "Paris in an Uproar, or Assault on the bastille" in which will be exhibited the Governor, Major, Gardes Criminelles and Gardes Françoises, Emblems of Liberty &c taken on the spot. The Scenery and Machinery painted and executed by Mr Ninham of this city.

This show was evidently popular, for in the following month, the rival concern Keymer's Vauxhall Gardens, offered for Assize week:

> The triumph of Liberty or Releasement from the Bastille—a picturesque view of the Bastille, the various instruments of torture, gloomy cells, skeletons, wretched victims chained in a variety of postures and liberated by the brave Henry Dubois,

the scenery being painted by Mr Keymer himself. Not to be outdone Quantrell improved on his performance, displaying, he said, all the instruments of cruelty, skeletons of those who were starved to death in iron cages, the beheading of the Governor, the uniform of the Major—with new choruses adapted to the piece.

Meanwhile French finances were in difficulty and foodstuffs were short. William Windham supported measures taken in parliament for shipping corn to France. He realised that this would not be universally popular with his constituents to whom cheap corn was of prime importance and he wrote to the Norwich papers to justify his position and point out that despite the ferment in France, Englishmen could travel there in perfect safety and indeed were received with particular cordiality as persons presumed to be well-affected to the cause of liberty for which the French were contending.[3]

When November came round again a second celebration of the anniversary of the Glorious Revolution was held and occasion was then taken to form a Revolution Society with William Taylor senior as secretary, an appointment which, we are told, gratified at once his taste for convivial pleasures and his attachment to the cause of civil and religious liberty. In fact his son of the same name seems to have been the power behind the throne and to have conducted the society's correspondence.[4] While the Revolution Society looked back to 1688, those who formed it undoubtedly had their eyes upon events in France as well.

In the same month that the Revolution Society was founded the Norwich dissenters held a meeting at the Maid's Head under the chairmanship of Alderman Elias Norgate, a member of the Presbyterian church at the Octagon. They declared themselves loyal subjects of the House of Brunswick but considered that every member of a civil society was entitled to participate in all its rights and privileges unless he had done anything to forfeit them. They therefore regarded it as a most unmerited indignity that they were excluded from places of trust and profit under the government and they once more sought the repeal of the Test and Corporation Acts. Their proceedings led to a correspondence in the Norwich papers. Some writers desired an even wider liberty to include Roman Catholics, while "country rector" asked whether "this sect" was really so quiet and innocent:

> Is it not rather aspiring with impudent ambition to overthrow both the hierarchy and monarchy of this kingdom and once more as under Cromwell to confound all subordination, all distinction of ranks, in democratic equality and to crumble the temple of the constitution into ruinous anarchy.[5]

When the petitions of the dissenters from various localities ultimately reached parliament, Charles James Fox proposed the repeal of the acts but it was opposed by Pitt and not carried.

The year 1790 opened hopefully. According to the *Norwich Mercury*, a further reduction of the armed forces was confidently spoken of, but by the Spring the climate had changed. Britain was in dispute with Spain over the settlement at Nootka in North America—"Everything breathes war throughout Europe".[6] Norwich was not prosperous and the Corporation, seeking means of retrenchment, resolved to pay off the City Waits, musicians whose history dated back into medieval times, and to dispense with the provision of wine at the Guildhall on days of rejoicing.[7]

Leaving these anxieties behind, William Taylor junior paid a visit to France. On 9 May at Calais he recorded that he had kissed the earth on the land of liberty. A few days later he wrote from Paris:

> I am at length in that point of space where the mighty sea of truth is in constant agitation and every billow dashes into fragments some deep-rooted rock of prejudice or buries in a viewless gulph some institution of gothic barbarism and superstition. I am at length in the neighbourhood of the National Assembly, that well-head of philosophical legislation whose pure streams are now overflowing the fairest country upon earth and will soon be sluiced off into the other realms of Europe, fertilising all with the living energy of its waters.

He wrote later describing the constant rattle of patriot drums the militia guarding every palace and stationed in every playhouse:

> It is like living in a citadel besieged. In every street you are surrounded by hawkers of pamphlets with terrific titles and every hour is startled with some new tale of terror.

He spent nine days in the National Assembly and heard all the eminent speakers, noting that when the question was foreseen the members made no scruple of reading their speeches upon the subject:

> Of the wisdom, talent and taste displayed in every decree emanating from the National Assembly I remain the most unqualified admirer, but that their conduct is governed by the lofty motives they profess is, I must think, extremely problematical. . . .

He noted that half the active citizens of France were illiterate; that four provinces were in a state of dangerous anarchy. 'It will be some years before rank recovers its stability and property its security in this country. . . .'

On his return William Taylor translated some of the decrees of the National Assembly and read them at a meeting of the Revolution Society.[8]

For Norwich citizens at home the local papers printed a constant flow of news items from France. Up to the spring of 1790 these reports still had a hopeful tone and emphasised the desire of the French to imitate the English. In March they reported that a French architect had been measuring every part of the House of Commons with a view to building a Senate House in Paris on the same plan. In April it was said that the French were to adopt "our trial by Jury" and in the next month that the National Assembly had asked the King to write to His Britannic Majesty with a view to establishing a universal standard of weights and measures, members of the Royal Society and the French Academy of Science to be asked to settle the details. At the end of May the decision of the National Assembly that the prerogative of declaring war and making peace should no longer rest with the king but be vested in the representatives of the people met with warm approbation. Said the *Norwich Mercury*:

> The ambition of the House of Bourbon has long been the source of war. Annihilate that and Great Britain, Spain, France, Portugal and Holland must long enjoy the Blessings of Peace.

REFERENCES

1. Lady Eastlake, *Dr Rigby's letters from France.*
2. M. H. Wilkin, *Joseph Kinghorn of Norwich,* p. 163.

3. *Norfolk Chronicle*, 8 August 1789.
4. J. W. Robberds, *Memoir of William Taylor*, p. 67.
5. *Norfolk Chronicle*, 21 Nov. 1789.
6. *Norwich Mercury*, 8 May 1790.
7. Norwich Assembly Book, 25 March 1790.
8. J. W. Robberds, op. cit., pp. 68–72.

3 Norwich Politics 1790–1792

The novelist, Ralph Mottram, brought up in a long family tradition of active participation in Norwich politics, writing in *The Boroughmonger*, gave an accurate description of the nature of the local parties as they had existed in the eighteenth century. Mr Varly of the reforming party is made to say:

> The Blue Party [he has transposed the colours; this truly refers to the Orange and Purples]—the Blue party represent solid interests which desire not to be disturbed. We on the other hand are composed of all those who desire a change. They are united in defence of one thing, the status quo; we are divided by our desire for something which does not yet exist, and which we therefore all see differently.

The French Revolution raised a new political awareness and aspiration amongst Norwich citizens. Yet the machinery of the two existing parties, the conservative Orange and Purples supporting Pitt and the government, and the reforming Blue and Whites looking to Fox and the opposition whigs, was able to contain the new energies, providing channels through which they could flow and not overflow.

Norwich returned two members to parliament and had one of the larger electorates in the country. The city's franchise was vested in the freeholders and the freemen. The latter were a large body to which admission could be obtained by birthright, by apprenticeship or by purchase. The Poll Book of the 1790 election records 2480 electors of whom 295 are said to be freeholders, the rest presumably freemen. The freemen annually elected the Common Council of the city. They also chose one of the two Sheriffs each year and when vacancies occurred they elected the Aldermen who served for life and from whom the Mayor was chosen.

C

Political attitudes are always coloured by past experience. Thus to understand the politics of the 1790s it is necessary to look back some years. A convenient starting point is the appearance of William Windham on the Norwich scene in January 1778, when he attended a meeting at the Maid's Head Inn called to raise a subscription towards the costs of the American war. He opposed the subscription, speaking of the conflict as an "unnatural, fruitless and ruinous war" and condemning the "folly, oppression and cruelty" which caused it.[1] Woodforde, who was present, noted that he spoke "exceeding well with great Fluency and Oratory, but on the wrong side".[2] This speech commended him to the Norwich radicals who invited him to stand for election to parliament in the 1780 election. There were three other candidates: Sir Harbord Harbord and Edward Bacon the sitting members, and John Thurlow, last year's Mayor and brother of the Lord Chancellor. In the event the sitting members were returned. Though bottom of the poll Windham polled over 1000 votes and the party had confidence in his future success. Alderman Norgate assured him of the "warm attachment of the inferior classes of freemen". The committee were anxious that he should declare himself "leader of the Independent interest" and when it came to an election they would bear a proportion of the expenses.[3] The election came in 1784.

Edward Bacon had died and there were three candidates for the two seats. No one doubted but that Sir Harbord Harbord would be at the top of the poll. The contest was effectively between William Windham and the Hon. Henry Hobart, who declared himself successor to Bacon in his zeal for the dignity of the crown. This time Windham won by a margin of 64 votes. When Harbord became Lord Suffield in 1786 Hobart stood again, now opposed by Sir Thomas Beevor, Bart., of Hethel in the Blue and White interest. The election was fiercely fought in a quite literal sense. There were two polling booths, one for each party, on the marketplace with a "no man's-land" between. At about five in the afternoon Beevor's stavesmen advanced with threatening aspect beyond their due bounds. A mutual defiance led to a mutual exchange of blows. The Sheriffs and their supporters succeeded in quelling the riot but Sheriff

Patteson was knocked down during the fracas by one of Beevor's stavesmen. The offender was arrested but later released being found "drunk and respectable". The poll was resumed next day and eventually Hobart was declared elected by 1450 votes to 1383.[4] Beevor petitioned against Hobart's return and the evidence given by some fifty witnesses before a committee of the Commons throws a flood of light on Norwich election habits. Hobart's agent had assembled Norwich freemen living in the metropolis at two inns in Spitalfields where they were provided with food and drink and then conveyed by coach to Swaffham in Norfolk. Understanding that Beevor had parties out on the usual routes into Norwich meaning to prevent them reaching the city, he kept them at Swaffham for eight days. Naturally they became disgruntled and talked of going over to Beevor but the agent, as he put it, took pains to keep them in temper. Hobart ultimately polled 107 London votes, Beevor 104.

No one would disclose exactly who had served on Hobart's committee and the publicans who had given free refreshments to voters denied having any precise instructions or keeping account of what they had supplied. It was however agreed that about £4000 had been spent on Hobart's behalf. Hobart's counsel called a number of witnesses who had worked for Beevor, the principal one being Mark Wilks the Baptist parson who was a great party worker. Wilks testified that he had told Sir Thomas that the freemen were desirous to have a little liquor and orders had been written for a few public houses to be opened for a number to have drinks to the value of 1s a night for two nights a week during the election period. Sir Thomas declared that the orders should not go out. Wilks told him that if he refused beer to the freemen he might as well go home and take no more trouble. He replied with an oath so he would then and went back to Hethel. These orders did not go out. Yet Beevor's supporters had spent over £3000. The committee found that a number of those whose votes had been recorded for Hobart were not in fact freemen, others were disqualified by reason of receiving parish relief or being resident in the workhouses or hospitals while 33 had been corrupted by bribery. The election was declared void and was fought again in March 1787. Again much money was spent in mobilising London voters—Hobart recorded 81, Beevor 93. In all Hobart polled 1393 and Beevor 1313 and this time Beevor accepted the result. Windham and Hobart were now the two members for Norwich and were to remain so till the death of the latter in 1799.

Windham's diaries tell something of the part he took in Norwich life. He dined with the Sheriffs and with the Mayor and Justices; he slept sometimes at the Bishop's Palace, more often at the William Taylors'. Though he often recorded his enjoyment of Norwich society he clearly felt himself superior to it—after dining with his supporters at Tuck's Coffee House in March 1789, "Felt as gay and happy as in better company".[5] But Henry Hobart succeeded in attaching to himself a personal following in a way that Windham did not. Probably he was prepared to take more trouble about the narrower interests of the city while Windham was more concerned with the broader needs of the nation. Engraved on his monument in Felbrigg church are the words "His views and counsels were directed more to raising the glory than increasing the wealth of his country". Norwich was certainly more interested in wealth— the merchants and manufacturers in the increase of their capital; the weavers and other tradesmen in a sufficient living wage as opposed to grinding poverty. So the majority of voters inclined to Hobart's views and the city was, as a writer expressed it some years later:

> Careless of Britain's weal or woe,
> While thy looms with yarn o'erflow.

When the 1790 election came on with its background of the ferment in France it was likely that Henry Hobart would head the poll. This being so the conflict was rather between the two Blue and White candidates, William Windham and Sir Thomas Beevor for the second seat than between him and them. In the event Beevor had little support—perhaps his petition in 1786 was resented. His supporters had rallied to him in 1787 and had he succeeded would no doubt have continued to do so but he had not succeeded. The voting this time was:

Hobart 1492   Windham 1361   Beevor 656.

It is interesting to note how the candidates themselves voted. Beevor plumped for himself; Hobart voted for himself and Windham while Windham bestowed a vote on each of his opponents.

That autumn there appeared a pamphlet which was to have far-reaching political consequences. Windham recorded in his diary on 7 November that he had received Mr Burke's pamphlet —the Reflections on the French Revolution. In lucid and eloquent prose Burke enforced the importance for freedom and order of the traditional elements of the British constitution, declared that France had substituted the despotism of the multitude for that of the monarch and pointed out that, with such a government, everything depended on the army. Windham who had previously supported the libertarian aspects of the revolution was wholly converted to Burke's view. He wrote:

> Never was there I suppose a work so valuable in its kind or that displayed powers of so extraordinary a nature. It is a work that may seem capable of overturning the National Assembly and turning the stream of opinion throughout Europe.[6]

A week later Windham came to Norwich to discuss with the manufacturers a Bill respecting wool. He realised that his views were diverging from those of his supporters on the issue of the Revolution but the matter did not arise and relations were "comfortable from memory of the election". He stayed at the Angel and went to a ball in the evening which proved sufficiently pleasant.[7]

Burke's pamphlet was answered in March 1791 by Tom Paine's "Rights of Man" and a month later by James Mackintosh's "Vindiciae Gallicae". Paine was an East Anglian, born at Thetford while Mackintosh was well known to Norwich whigs as a visitor to the city when he came to plead at the Assizes. As we shall see both these works were to exercise a considerable influence in Norwich.

In 1791 foreign politics once more caused anxiety. Catherine was said to be trying to establish a navy for Russia that would challenge the British fleet. Once more there were rumours of

war and fears for the effect it would have on Norwich commerce. In April a Common Hall of citizens was summoned to
make a petition against going to war with Russia. Jeremiah
Ives junior, who said that the labour cost on goods made for
Russia last winter had amounted to £20,000, moved a series of
propositions:

> 1. The principal support of the City of Norwich derives
> from the export of manufactures. Russian demand affords
> support to a numerous body of the poor.
> 2. If there is war with Russia these poor will be nearly
> destitute.
> 3. The expence of their maintenance will fall on inhabi-
> tants of the city already oppressed by national and local
> taxes.
> 4. War can only be justified on principles of self-
> defence; to involve nations mutually beneficial to each
> other is not consistent with the principles of humanity or
> sound policy.

Robert Harvey agreed with Ives as to the facts but argued
against a petition which might embarrass His Majesty's
Ministers in their negotiations. He also pointed out that
whereas the Russians received prompt payment for their
produce, our goods were sent there "at risque and long credit".
The meeting passed the resolutions and agreed to send them
to the local Members of Parliament and the Norwich, London
and Manchester newspapers.[8] In the House Windham spoke
against a war saying that Norwich manufacturers dreaded the
utter ruin of their trade. Despite the danger of war and the risk
of long credit the Norwich merchants were still willing to trade
with Russia. Only a fortnight later the *Norfolk Chronicle*
reported a great export of Norwich stuffs including two ship-
loads to Petersburgh.[9]

Events in France were polarising Norwich politics. On
Thursday 14 July, being the second anniversary of the fall of
the Bastille, enthusiasts for the Revolution gave up the day to
celebration. In the morning and afternoon Mark Wilks held
services in St Paul's chapel and preached resounding sermons
on "The Origins and Stability of the French Revolution" from

the text in Acts V, 39, "If it be of God ye cannot overthrow it". He criticised Burke's "Reflections" and quoted freely from Paine's "Rights of Man". The National Assembly, he held, was one where mercy and truth met together. They wreaked their rage against principles not persons, against tyranny not tyrants—men whose government had never been stained with one drop of human blood. This was the introduction of a government of which reason was the author and utility the object, a government reared on the immutable basis of natural right and general happiness, combining all the excellencies and excluding all the defects of other constitutions. The ruin of England had been inevitable but for the revolution in France. His Majesty and his servants must admire a revolution that prevents one here.[10]

The evening after this feast of oratory a numerous and respectable company dined expensively—6s a head—at the Maid's Head Inn and drank fifteen toasts including:

> Perfection and stability to a free Constitution for France.
>
> The Philosophers of France and may the diffusion of political knowledge instruct the ignorant and silence the interested.
>
> The rights of man and the rights of nations—may the best governments be reformed and the worst regenerated.
>
> The English authors who have vindicated the French Revolution.
>
> The friends of liberty all the world over.[11]

This enthusiasm for things French naturally provoked a reaction. A week later the "Friends of the Constitution" dined at Keymer's Pavilion with John Harvey in the chair and drank to "The King", "The Constitution", "Mr Pitt and the Administration", "Mr Hobart" and "Mr Burke".[12]

While these peaceful manifestations of opinion were going on in Norwich, a mob in Birmingham, stirred up to hatred of the revolution and its sympathisers was wrecking Meeting Houses and burning down the dwelling and library of the eminent scientist and dissenting divine, Dr Joseph Priestley. On this news reaching Norwich one of the Martineau family invited a number of gentlemen to supper to consider making

a public tribute to the Doctor and a plan to alleviate his distress.[13] These were violent days and Norwich was not altogether
immune. In October the papers reported "a violent outrage on
public decency"—four men rode furiously through Magdalen
St and with their whips broke all the lamps and several shop
windows, the damage amounting to about £100.[14] But then
mere vandalism was less dangerous than violence with serious
political intent.

By the end of 1791 the *Norwich Mercury* had passed over from
enthusiastic approval of the Revolution to a grudging hope
that at some time in the remote future "from partial evil,
general good may arise".[15]

At the beginning of the year 1792 the weaving trade was
pretty busy and leading citizens found time to give thought to
the troubles of the world. A numerous and respectable meeting
on 8 February unanimously agreed to a petition to the Commons
against the African Slave Traffic and when the Quarterly
Assembly of the Corporation met later in the month they drew
up a parallel petition for the abolition of a trade "so disgraceful
to a Christian country and incompatible with the sentiments
or feelings of humanity". Many citizens resolved totally to
abstain from the use of sugar as an efficacious way of securing
the abolition of the trade. In March the Revolution Society
voted a subscription of £10 10s od to the anti-slave-trade
committee, while a vote in the Commons on 2 April in favour
of gradual abolition was greeted by the ringing of St Peters'
bells two days running and, said the *Norfolk Chronicle*, the
general joy of the citizens in the triumph of humanity.[16] This
euphoria was short lived for the proposal was unacceptable to
Wilberforce and the protagonists of instant abolition and so
proved abortive.

In April 1792 the Norwich Revolution Society wrote to the
London Society for Constitutional Information seeking an
association with them. The London Society, which had been
founded in 1780, had recently been divided between supporters
of the views of Tom Paine and those of the more conservative
reformer, Christopher Wyvill, who accused Paine of offering
the lower classes the prospect of plundering the rich. The
Painites were at this time gaining control. The Norwich society

asked to be allowed to nominate twelve members to that in London. They would be willing to circulate information and to co-operate in measures to further the cause of Parliamentary reform. The principles and opinions of their society, they said, were best expressed in Mackintosh's "Vindiciae Gallicae" except that they dissented from his opinion that there were two interests in society, those of the rich and those of the poor— "If so what chance have the latter?"—surely the interests of all the industrious in the community are the same: to lessen the number of unproductive and to do away with such impositions and imposts as abridge the means of maintenance. To this end they desired an equitable representation of the people. Their members, they said, undertook an annual obligation to contribute towards the purchase of books to circulate among confederated clubs—there were seven of these at present and more were expected. At this time Thomas Goff was President of the Society and John Cozens had succeeded William Taylor as Secretary. The leadership had passed from the merchant aristocracy of the city to the shopkeeping class—both Goff and Cozens were grocers.

The London Association evidently made enquiries as to the status of the nominees proposed to them. Horne Tooke noted descriptions against several of the names thus:

William Taylor . . . one of the first manufacturers
William Firth . . . a considerable manufacturer
Thomas Barnard . . . a considerable manufacturer
Mark Wilks . . . preacher
Edward Barrow . . . a considerable warehouseman

Other nominees were Charles Basham, a snuff-maker, John Dalrymple, a brandy merchant of Norwich, Henry Dobson, an architect and builder who a few months later decided to migrate to France, and George Watson who though he lived at Saxlingham was a member of the Baptist church in St Mary's Norwich.[17]

In May 1792 the *Norfolk Chronicle* was complaining of a long continued north east wind destructive of vegetation and hoping for a fine warm rain to produce a happy change in favour of the poor. The government had other anxieties and the King issued a proclamation against the printing and dispersal of seditious writings calculated to overturn the Constitution "whence we derive the blessings of rational freedom with the protection of property". Magistrates were urged to seek out the authors of such writings and to suppress them.

By the autumn the full employment of the beginning of the year had declined and the price of bread advanced. The mayor, sheriffs and aldermen on 24 October resolved on a petition to His Majesty in Council pointing out that bread corn had lately been exported from Norfolk ports and prices had rapidly risen giving cause to apprehend the most alarming consequences. They prayed for a temporary prohibition on the export of wheat.[18]

The events in France were such that home anxieties could not keep them out of mind. The papers carried lurid accounts of the September massacres. The effect of these happenings on English opinion was succinctly defined by an eminent Scottish lawyer:

> All ordinary faction was absorbed by two parties—of those who thought that the terrible example by shewing the danger of wrongs too long maintained, was the strongest reason for the timely correction of our own defects,—and of those who considered this opinion as a revolutionary device and held that the attrocities in France were conclusive against our exciting sympathetic hopes by any admission that curable defect existed.[19]

Thus the reformers, however much they might deplore the atrocities in Paris, were unchanged in their view of what was wanted at home, while the horrors moved the opponents of reform to a fresh enthusiasm.

John Harvey, who was mayor this year, was one of the tory persuasion and was determined to turn the anniversary of the Glorious Revolution, which two years before had been the occasion of forming the Revolution Society, to good account. Accordingly the mayor, sheriffs and aldermen passed a resolution in support of the constitution and calling on all citizens to assist the magistrates in enforcing the law. The same evening the mayor presided at a dinner at the King's Head when the toasts included:

> May the seeds of sedition never take root in British soil.
> May Pain be expelled from every British bosom.[20]

Mr Hobart and Mr Windham were also toasted, indicating that the latter was now seen to be detached from the supporters of the Revolution.

The following Tuesday the mayor presided over another meeting at the Maid's Head called on the requisition of several gentlemen. He spoke of combinations of wicked and designing men who:

> Disperse innumerable handbills and cheap publications, the false reasonings of which are meant to delude and ensnare the lower class of the people, from whose useful labours our manufactures thrive and commerce flourishes. Missionaries are sent from club to club to disseminate these detestable opinions that the poison of sedition may be more copiously diffused.[21]

A declaration of support to the constitution and government by King, Lords and Commons and for support for the laws which have hitherto preserved the Liberty, protected the property and increased the enjoyments of a free and prosperous people, was carried unanimously and a committee of 25 was appointed to obtain signatures of citizens. But this did not terminate the proceedings. The Rev. Gee Smyth moved to open a subscription to supply provisions and coals at reduced prices to the industrious poor, distressed by the scarcity of work and high level of prices. Alderman Robert Harvey trusted that benevolence would always be the handmaid of British loyalty and that the worthy poor man might pass his winter's evenings by his own comfortable fireside, cheerful with his family and grateful for the blessings he enjoys. This won unanimous support and in due course the mayor was chosen treasurer and a committee set up on a territorial basis including representatives from the other side of politics. By the new year upwards of £1700 had been subscribed.

Apart from his political activities John Harvey was an

important figure in Norwich industry. He introduced the manufacture of shawls for which the city was to become famous. He was popular with the weavers who presented an address to him at the end of his mayoral year expressing their happiness that his heart was open to the distresses of the poor and to their just complaints.

At this time Charles Harvey, younger brother of the mayor, was Steward of Norwich and in that capacity delivered a charge to the grand jury drawing attention to the offences of publishing and circulating seditious and inflammatory libels with a view to overturning the constitution. He waxed eloquent upon the state of France, a tyranny far more dreadful and alarming than their former despotism:

> Good God, gentlemen, he concluded, when acts from which all mankind shrinks in horror are not only palliated and excused, but when the perpetrators of them are openly espoused and countenanced, it is natural for men to enquire into the views and motives of their advocates. . . .[22]

These strong reactions from the right were perhaps called forth by the spread of political activity in a different class of citizens from the well-to-do members of the Revolution Society. That November Isaac Saint, publican of the Weaver's Arms in St Augustines, Anthony Cadywould, a cordwainer, and one George Knapp wrote to the London Corresponding Society in the name of the Norwich Society for Political Information asking to be incorporated in "your worthy fraternity". The London society, which was on a more popular basis than the Society for Constitutional Information, was founded early in 1792 by Thomas Hardy, a shoemaker of Piccadilly, its members subscribing a penny a week towards the costs of corresponding with like-minded groups in the country. The Norwich correspondents commented that the various societies did not seem to agree in their objectives, some wanting reform on the Duke of Richmond's plan*, some to rip up monarchy by the roots and plant democracy in its place.

---

* Charles Lennox, third Duke of Richmond (1735–1806) in June 1780 had brought forward in Parliament his Reform Bill providing for annual parliaments, manhood suffrage and equal electoral districts. It was rejected without a division.

Their society favoured full and equal representation, general suffrage and annual parliaments.[23]

This letter drew a reply from Maurice Margarot who pointed out that the London Corresponding Society had never heard of their society before. Although Margarot said nothing of it, they had been in correspondence with the Norwich Revolution Society a month earlier, asking support for a friendly address to the French National Convention.[24] They would therefore, he said, want more information on its origins, principles and numbers. He advised them to leave monarchy, democracy and even religion aside and to try to increase support for equal representation of the people in parliament, leaving the parliament so chosen, to plan remedies for abuses. He understood there were many societies in Norwich and recommended them to unite. Also he suggested they should appoint one of the least conspicuous of their members to receive correspondence.

It would seem that the two streams of reforming activity in Norwich were in due time merged and Saint became secretary when Cozens ceased to act. Meanwhile, that December Cozens wrote to Thomas Hardy of the London Corresponding Society, regarding the Mayor's initiative. Meetings were being held to declare attachment to the present constitution of the country and a declaration was being carried from door to door for signature. "Would your societies sign?" Hardy promptly replied that not one of his members would sign such a declaration.[25] Cozens wrote again on Christmas day saying that the Norwich magistrates had not as yet interfered with the publicans—that is to say the licencees of inns where meetings of the confederated societies were held.

Windham now made his position clear in Parliament. A supplement to the *Norfolk Chronicle* on 22 December 1792 reported his speech supporting the Ministry in calling out the militia. He should vote, he said, with those whose measures he had uniformly and conscientiously reprobated. There had been constant communication between persons in London and Paris with the object of destroying our present form of government. Pamphlets against the British Constitution were disseminated in every town and village, supported, he believed, by a purse made up in France. He saw no great loss to society in putting an end to public house political clubs and ale house debates on politics.

Henceforth his former supporters referred to him as Weathercock Windham.

Meanwhile a Norwich character of a very different stamp was an eye-witness of some of the tragic events in France. Col John Money had inherited a small estate on the borders of Norwich, renaming it Crown Point after a battle in which he had taken part in the American war. Money was well known in Norwich society. He was wont to give an annual ball which was patronised by leading citizens and he seems to have kept up relationships with people of both political persuasions. He was an occasional visitor to Earlham, and Elizabeth Gurney, writing a few years later than this, recorded in her journal her pleasure at meeting him, though, she told herself, "It is better to overlook such people as him who are so fasenating and not good characters. . . ." This comment perhaps related to the fact that though not married Money was the father of two sons.

John Money was a professional soldier and seeing no prospect of service under the English Crown was glad enough to comply with an invitation to raise a legion for the French army which came to him in the spring of 1792. The National Assembly passed a decree allowing four foreign generals to be taken into service—a decree which Money said was passed solely on his account. He reached France in July 1792 and received his commission as Maréchal des Camps et Armées. He was in Paris at his Hôtel in the rue Petit Piére on the night of 9 August, when he was wakened by an aide-de-camp who told him that the Marseillois and the mob of St Antoine were going to attack the Thuilleries intending to massacre the royal family. They put on their uniforms and went out finding the streets empty despite the noise of drums beating to arms. Reaching the Thuilleries they went up to the royal apartments where they found nearly a hundred officers gathered. At six in the morning they were told that the King intended to go to the Assembly for protection. Money set off for the Assembly but could not gain admission. He took off his epaulettes and returned to Paris. He found the streets crowded and saw a mob carrying on pikes and bayonets the heads of the Swiss Guards who had been butchered at the Thuilleries. After this he said he tried to arrange to return to England but found it prudent to soldier on, fighting against the Austrians in Belgium. In December he was offered promotion to Lieutenant General but concluding that war with England was now inevitable and fearing the imputation of serving the enemy, he resigned his commission.[26] On 23 December he wrote to the Norwich papers that he had that morning sent his resignation to the Conventional Assembly:

> When I engaged to serve these people they had a King and Constitution; now they have neither—they are all mad and the army think so.[27]

Tradition tells that Money obtained a passport to England for himself and a servant. Young Hudson Gurney was in France and could not get one. Money paid off his French valet and brought Gurney home in his livery.

REFERENCES

 1. R. W. Ketton-Cremer, *Early Life and Diaries of Wm. Windham,* 1930, p. 187.
 2. *Diary of a Country Parson,* vol. 1, p. 217.
 3. R. W. Ketton-Cremer, op. cit., p. 211.
 4. *Norwich Mercury,* 23 Sept. 1786.
 5. Mrs Baring, *Diary of the Rt. Hon. Wm. Windham,* 1866, p. 167.
 6. Mrs Baring, op. cit., p. 213.
 7. Mrs Baring, op. cit., p. 213.
 8. *Norfolk Chronicle,* 30 April 1791.
 9. *Norfolk Chronicle,* 14 May 1791.
10. Mark Wilks. Two sermons preached 14 July 1791 on the origin and stability of the French Revolution.
11. *Norwich Mercury,* 9, 16 July 1791.
12. *Norfolk Chronicle,* 23 July 1791.
13. Joseph Kinghorn's Correspondence.
14. *Norwich Mercury,* 22 Oct. 1791.
15. *Norwich Mercury,* 10 Dec. 1791.
16. *Norfolk Chronicle,* 7 April 1792.
17. *Complete Collection of State Trials,* vol. XXV, p. 148.
18. Norwich Court of Mayoralty Book, 24 Oct. 1792.
19. Lord Cockburn, *Life of Lord Jeffrey,* 1852, p. 73.
20. *Norfolk Chronicle,* 8 Dec. 1792.

21. *Norfolk Chronicle*, 15 Dec. 1792.
22. Charge to the Grand Jury of the City and County of Norwich, 18 Jan. 1793.
23. *State Trials*, vol. XXIV, p. 392.
24. Public Record Office, TS 24/10/10.
25. Public Record Office, TS 24/10/19.
26. J. Money, *History of the Campaign of 1792 between France and the Allies*, 1794.
27. *Norfolk Chronicle*, 5 Jan. 1793.

4 Norwich Politics 1793–1794

In January 1793 the Norwich papers reported the debate in the French Assembly on the judgment of the king. Tom Paine had appeared at the tribune and argued that the only ally of the Republic was the United States who considered themselves indebted to Louis for their liberty. It would therefore be politic to banish the king to America. Paine did not speak French so his speech had to be interpreted. No heed was paid to it. The king was condemned. The *Norwich Mercury* reported:

> Louis died with the most heroic fortitude. He was dressed in a brown great-coat, white waistcoat, black breaches and stockings. His hair was dressed.

A fortnight or so later the French declared war on Britain. These events could not but be inimical to the cause of reformers in England. Their approval of developments in France was now held to be unpatriotic and even treasonable. On the other hand their opposition to the war was likely to engender support in Norwich, for war was always bad for Norwich trade. As soon as recruiting started the hostility of the populace was manifest. Early in March one Captain Allen, raising an independent company, was trying to march his recruits out of the city when he was interrupted by "divers persons" who tried to prevent the march, sought to induce the recruits to disobedience and actually laid hold of them and threw stones.[1]

In the atmosphere then prevailing it was easy for unfounded alarms to arise. Windham, speaking in the House at the end of February 1793, said he had heard a report of clubs whose members received money for attendance and were told their services would be wanted on a future occasion.[2] The press improved on the story and David Kinghorn wrote from Yorkshire:

> I was struck at reading in the Doncaster Newspaper

D

that the Weavers of Norwich had 8 shillings a week paid
them while they attended at Clubs and Alehouses &c and
being asked why they did not work, answered they had
that paid them to be ready on a Call. If this is True, you
must have had some Sons of Belial among you who have
been endeavouring to blow up the Coals of Dissention in
a flame and bring England into the same miserable condition with france.

Joseph Kinghorn replied:

The account in the Doncaster paper you mention I have
every reason to believe is a downright *lie*! . . . there are
people enough in Norwich to have propagated such a
circumstance with pleasure but no such suspicion was
even heard here. . . . Norwich has been all along very *quiet*
—sentiments have been various & violent on all sides but
the parties were so balanced that quietness has been the
effect.

About this time the government, worried over possible
political developments in Norwich, obtained a report from a
Mr Alderton from which it appears that the Revolution Society
had become merged with the Bell Corporation Club. This was a
convivial club of long standing which met at the Bell Inn and
annually appointed a "Mayor" and other officers. Its minute
book records that in 1792 the club came under the shadow of
the "great events then passing" and found so great differences
of political sentiment among its members that they could no
longer meet in harmony. Those attached to whig "or even
French" principles continued at the Bell while the supporters of
Mr Pitt and the government crossed the road to the Castle Inn.
The club at the Bell, according to Mr Alderton, consisted of a
number of inferior tradesmen and three or four merchant
manufacturers. The most active member was "one Cozens, a
grocer in the market-place" and "among the better sort" one
William Barnard, a merchant of St George's Colegate, the
Messrs Taylors, Gough a grocer and Watson, the miller of
Saxlingham, a man of considerable property. There were forty
subsidiary clubs composed of persons of the lowest description,

numbering it was said, upwards of four thousand. The Bell club regularly appointed visitors to these clubs to inform them of its correspondence with societies in London and elsewhere. On a recent evening more than one hundred had assembled in Postle's cellar to hear readings from Mr Paine's Rights of Man. There were also affiliated societies in every town and almost every village in Norfolk.[3]

The accuracy of Alderton's report is born out by other evidence. As regards activity in the villages, Fanny Burney staying at Aylsham in 1792, noted:

> I am truely amazed to find this country filled with little revolution societies which transmit their notions to the larger committee at Norwich which communicates the whole to the reformists in London. I am told there is scarce a village in Norfolk free from these meetings.[4]

In June 1793 "Inhabitant of Horsford" wrote to the *Norwich Mercury* complaining of the activities of "Jacobin emissaries from Norwich" tampering with the principles of the villagers.

Norwich was a likely market for radical pamphlets. Early in May 1793 Joseph Kinghorn received a letter from Robert Hall* of Cambridge asking him to recommend a bookseller for his pamphlet, "An Apology for the Freedom of the Press and for General Liberty". It contained, he said, nothing dangerous or violent. The pamphlet was in fact an indictment of the status quo and an attack on the government which was not likely to please the establishment. Kinghorn, who was by no means a political activist, endorsed the letter with a note that he had ordered three dozen copies.

During the spring and summer of 1793 the Norwich radicals kept up a correspondence with the London Corresponding Society. In March, describing themselves as the United Political Societies, they wrote to London saying that they favoured universal suffrage and annual elections and asking what was "the sense of the people" collected by the corresponding

---

* The Rev. Robert Hall was a Baptist minister, famous for the eloquence of his preaching. At Aberdeen University he had been the close friend of James Mackintosh, the author of "Vindiciae Gallicae".

societies as to practical measures to be taken—a petition to
Parliament, an address to the King or a Convention? London
replied that they considered a convention most desirable and
that it would be practicable so soon as the great body of the
people should be courageous and virtuous enough to join in
the attempt.[5]

As soon as war had been declared the King proclaimed a
general Fast-day to be held on 19 April. This was duly observed.
Shops were shut. The Dragoons and Leicestershire Militia
paraded to St Peter's. Divine Service was performed in most
churches. Many collections were taken for the distressed
emigré clergy. The Mayor and principal gentlemen of the
corporation attended the cathedral where the Rev. Prebendary
Potter preached on the text "Fear God, honour the King",
taking occasion to inveigh against "The Rights of Man" by
which liberal code treason, rebellion, sacrilege, plunder and
the most horrid murders were sanctified.[6] Services were also
held in the principal dissenting meeting houses though the task
of their ministers was more difficult as they were generally
opposed to the war. Joseph Kinghorn wrote of it:

> Is the nation to be commanded to pray for the success
> of our Arms that their prayers may aid the designs of those
> who regard not God not consider the operation of his
> hands? Can we wish the destruction of a people who have
> just risen from slavery and on whose existence perhaps
> the freedom of Europe depends?

He took the precaution of writing out his sermon, taking his
text from Isaiah—"My counsel shall stand and I will do all my
pleasure". He was, he said, determined that no one should
know his political sentiments from his sermon.

From all parts of the country that spring came petitions for
the reform of Parliament. In the House of Commons Henry
Hobart produced the Norwich petition with upwards of 3700
signatures on eighteen large sheets of paper but he doubted if
it could be received as the names were subscribed to a printed
copy. The Speaker, citing a precedent of 1656, ruled against it
but as there were similar petitions from other quarters the
matter was debated. Windham made a long and ingenious

speech against reform. There were, he said, three kinds of majority—of reason, of number and of force. The good looked for a majority of reason and of force: the bad of force only. A majority of numbers was of little consequence. A majority of force had influenced the sanguinary and detestable proceedings at Paris and he feared the same effects here. The debate occupied two days, dragging on till 4am when 282 members voted against committing the petitions and only 41 in favour.[7] The *Norfolk Chronicle* thought the matter of sufficient local interest to publish a supplement on it.

If some Norwich radicals had followed Windham and moved to the right, others were inclined to adopt a more extreme position. H. Buckle, a breeches maker, writing in June 1793 to the London Corresponding Society on behalf of the Norwich societies, wholly abandoned the old position of the Revolution Society which had equated the interests of the richest merchant and the poorest mechanic. Where, he asked, was the majesty of the people? An indifferent observer would suppose it to centre in stars and garters, ribbons and costly apparel, places, coaches and horses, with all the trumpery of puerile amusements. Were it not for their accursed consequences they could bear with it, but when they considered how many toiled and starved to support it, how could they be persuaded but that there was a contrivance between the landowner and the merchant to hold the people in vassalage?[8]

The surrender of Valenciennes to the siege of the Duke of York at the end of July was an occasion for rejoicing for loyal citizens—all but a few rank Jacobins, said the *Norwich Mercury*. The Newmarket mail coach brought the news, its driver and guard wearing cockades and discharging fire arms. A flag was run up on St Peter's tower; a 50 stone bullock roasted in Ber Street and its meat distributed to the populace with upwards of 2000 penny loaves and four barrels of beer. Bells were rung and houses decorated with flags and streamers while a band played The Roast Beef of Old England and God Save the King. Even in so poor a parish as St Martin's at Oak the clerk proudly entered in his accounts, otherwise made up of the purchase of brushes, dwiles and candles, the cost of cleaning and small repairs and the purchase of beer for those who did them:

> Paid the Ringers on Account of the Surrender of
> Valencies to His Royal Highness the Duke of York—7/6.

Windham had been on a visit to the troops at Valenciennes
at the time of its surrender. By September he was home and
entertained John Harvey and John Gurney, leading members
of the opposite political factions in Norwich, to dinner at
Felbrigg—both happened to be holidaying at Cromer.[9] In
October he wrote that his hostility to Jacobinism and all its
works and all its supporters, whether weak or wicked, was
steady and strong and if Pitt were the man to oppose it he
should stand by Pitt.[10] He paid some attention to his consti-
tuency that autumn. On 9 October he dined at the Swan and
went to a ball which was distinguished by the presence of
Mrs Siddons. Next day he dined with the bishop and some
fifty others mostly clergy and in the evening went to Col
Money's ball. Then on the 11th he dined with the sheriffs at
the King's Head. He noted that John Robinson, the former
sheriff, was "more to talk to than the generality" of those he
met on such occasions. Alas, Robinson was to vote against him
in the next election. He noted in his diary how low were the
talents and understanding of nearly all who composed Norwich
society and, by a curious contrast, "the French are a more
generally polished and enlightened people". On the 12th he
drank tea with William Unthank, an old supporter who was
to support him no longer, and went to Thomas Harvey's at
Catton where Mrs Siddons was reading a play. Mrs Siddons
was at home here, her sister being the wife of Mrs Harvey's
brother. Later in the month Windham was back in the city
dining with the mayor, John Buckle, who had voted for him
before and would continue to do so. On 19 November he was
back again to dine with several of his old supporters—Barnard,
Ives, Rigby, William Taylor junior and Martineau. Little
politics were talked save what they forced on. The fear of being
too polemic held him back, which he afterwards regretted.[11]
Of his companions on this occasion only Ives was to spare him
a vote at the next election and Ives did not support him thereafter.

Delegates of the Societies of Friends of the People in

Scotland had been meeting as a Convention in Edinburgh at
intervals since December 1792. One of the leaders of the movement was Lord Daer who had been the schoolfellow of William
Taylor and Frank Sayers at Mrs Barbauld's school at Palgrave,
a nursery of radical opinions. In the autumn of 1793 this
Scottish Convention of Friends of the People resolved to open
correspondence with all such societies in the kingdom. This
seemed to open a prospect of holding in Edinburgh the desired
convention aimed at securing the reform of Parliament. The
Norwich societies appointed Maurice Margarot, one of the
London delegates, to represent them. The English delegates
were some days late and when they got to Edinburgh on 6
November, found the Convention adjourned. It was got
together again on 19 November and assumed the name of the
British Convention of the Friends of the People associated to
obtain universal suffrage and annual parliaments. After debate
the convention published an address in which it declared that
the throne was endangered by evil ministers who encouraged
the king to emulate James II. If the teaching of the Prince of
Peace were followed the national debt would be alleviated and
commerce and manufactures would flourish. The sole aim of
the convention was declared to be the "restoration" of annual
parliaments and universal suffrage.[12] Early in December its
leaders were arrested and the convention broken up. Margarot
was subsequently tried on a charge of sedition and sentenced
to fourteen years transportation. Meanwhile in Norwich a
minor sensation had arisen from the posting up of seditious
hand-bills. The text of one as printed in the *Norwich Mercury*
of 2 November 1793 read:

"To all real Lovers of Liberty. My Friends and Fellow
Citizens.

It is with the greatest Joy I congratulate you on the
Defeat of the combined Tyrants—Be assured that Liberty
and Freedom will at least prevail. Tremble O thou
Oppresser of the People that reigneth upon the Throne,
and ye Ministers of State, Weep for ye shall fall, Weep oh
ye Conductors of this vile and wicked War, ye who grind
the Face of the Poor, oppress the People, and starve the

Industrious Mechanic—My Friends, you are oppressed,
you know it—Revenge it. Lord Buckingham who died
the other Day, had Thirty Thousand Pounds yearly for
setting his Arse in the House of Lords, and doing nothing
—Think of this, ye who work hard, and have hardly a
Crust to put in your Mouths, think how many wretches it
would have made happy, in short my Friends Liberty calls
aloud, ye who will hear her Voice may you be free and
happy, He who does not let him starve and be damned.
Sunday, Sept. 14th.

N.B. Be resolute and ye shall be happy. He who wishes
well to the cause of Liberty, let him repair to Chapel Field
at Five o'clock this afternoon to begin a Glorious
Revolution."

The contemplated glorious revolution never began. £200
was offered by the lords commissioners of the Treasury for the
conviction of one or more of the offenders and the Court of
the Mayoralty promised an additional £100. The government
was sufficiently alarmed to send a solicitor down from London
to track down the authors but though he employed six night-
watchmen he was wholly unsuccessful.[13] It seems unlikely that
those responsible intended any more than a gesture of defiance.
Joseph Kinghorn wrote of the incident that a few copies were
written, one or more stuck up, the rest snatched up as curios-
ities—"it furnished a little conversation for the day".[14]

Norwich as a centre of population was required to do its
part in providing men for active service. Able bodied young
men were liable to be drawn by lot to serve in the militia
though it was possible to insure against this at W. T. Robberd's
stationery shop in the market place. A premium of 7s 6d
insured for one year the sum of £10 to anyone on whom the
lot fell and with this he could buy out his obligation. In
November Lieut Marsh arrived in Norwich with orders to
press men for the navy. The city fathers were by no means
willing to have press gangs operating here and to avoid this
they offered bounties of three guineas for suitable volunteers.
This led to at least nine men being enlisted.[15] At the same time
the Royal Artillary was trying to recruit young men of good

character and 5ft 7ins tall from the city. The pay offered was
6s 5d a week for a gunner with the added inducements of free
quarters and genteel clothing.[16] A few weeks later the authorities
offered the rank of Major to W. Earle Bulwer if he could raise a
company of 130 men. He offered ten guineas to a satisfactory
recruit and two more to anyone introducing such.[17] In May
1794 his effort was enlarged and adopted by the city. The
mayor's court wrote to Lord Amherst, commanding His
Majesty's forces, saying that Bulwer was now willing to raise a
corps of six hundred men under the city's auspices to be called
the Royal Norwich Volunteers.[18] They secured approval for
this plan and the Norwich or 106th Regiment of Foot when
raised was sent to Ireland and stationed near Waterford.
According to a tradition handed down in his family Bulwer cut
down the avenues of oak at his home at Heydon to raise the
money required to pay the bounties to his volunteers.

In November 1793 trade was bad and the *Chronicle* recommended city ladies to wear nothing but Norwich manufactures
and to ensure that their servants and dependants were similarly
clothed. The paper reported that the Dean's lady and several
others in the Close had adopted this plan. Then a subscription
was raised towards supplying flannel waistcoats to the troops
in Flanders and the Castle Corporation raised sufficient to
purchase one hundred. Besides this the manufacture was
especially recommended for funerals.

With the increasing cost of provisions the city's poor rate
this year reached the unprecedented figure of £19,559. Yet
Norwich benefitted from being the centre of an agricultural
district. At Christmas 1793 no less than 2550 turkeys were
shipped from Norwich to London in various conveyances.
Their average weight was 12 lb each and the price 8s.[19]

Fresh anxieties arose in the early months of 1794 when it
was learned that the Empress of Russia had prohibited the
import of worsteds. The manufacturers, relying on the com-
mercial treaty lately concluded with St Petersburg, had put in
hand work for the first spring ships, work which would be
unsaleable except on the Russian market. They applied to the
city's Members of Parliament to try to get the treaty imple-
mented.[20]

Meanwhile the Norwich Political Societies, unabashed by the treatment meted out to the conventionists in Edinburgh, published a defiant paper headed Declarations and Resolutions of the United Constitutional Societies at Norwich and dated 16 Jan 1794. They declared that the British Convention of delegates for Parliamentary Reform had by their conduct justly merited their approbation and that the Magistrates of Edinburgh had acted unconstitutionally against the persons of Margarot and his colleagues. They said that their rights under the Revolution settlement of 1688 had been invaded by various Acts of Parliament, in particular:

(1) The Bounty Act for exporting grain which had led to the neglect of rearing live stock and the reduction of industrious husbandmen to poverty.

(2) Government borrowing whereby £9,000,000 interest had to be found annually.

(3) The limitation of voting rights to people of property.

(4) The Septennial Act whereby Parliament has acquired unlimited power.

They considered they had a right to participate in the management of government and that it was their duty to form peaceable, rational and regular societies to investigate its principles. They wished their grievances redressed by meliorating the conditions of the labouring poor who could be relieved by the abolition of sinecures and unnecessary pensioners and reducing the number of placemen. They wanted universal suffrage, annual elections and such reform as was advocated by Mr Pitt in 1782. The paper was signed by J. Bagg as chairman and J. Saint,* secretary.[21] Of Saint, who was a publican, we shall hear more. According to his testimony Bagg was a working man who had read a lot of history. His chairmanship perhaps indicates that the better-to-do radicals had taken fright at this juncture. A meeting was held in February which unanimously resolved to send at least one delegate to the next General Convention called by the London society. "Many of our friends are fully convinced of the Necessity, Legality and

* This J. is assumed to be a printer's error; the reference is surely to Isaac Saint.

Rationality of a Convention but Quere whether the time be expedient".[22]

The Norwich societies took thought for Maurice Margarot, their unfortunate representative now on board ship at Spithead awaiting transportation and sent him £20. Acknowledging the gift he wrote them an extremely injudicious letter which was inevitably intercepted by the authorities:

> ... it is here reported that the Brest fleet is out: rumour ... says there are 70 sail of French at sea. If so there must be a number of transports among them and a descent may probably be the consequence. For God's sake my worthy friends do not relax in the cause of freedom ... consolidate your societies—unite with others—persevere, and make no doubt that sooner or later your endeavours will be crowned with success.[23]

In April 1794 when the Norfolk landowners met at the Shirehall to make plans for strengthening the war effort, John Barnard of Norwich ventured to say a few words on the distress occasioned by the war to those dependent on manufactures. A resolution to form volunteer companies was seconded by Windham who was interrupted by "the noisy intemperance of a few ignorant people".[24]

At this juncture the government decided on drastic action. On 12 May Thomas Hardy, secretary of the London Corresponding Society, Horne Tooke, John Thelwall and other London admirers of the Revolution, were arrested on the capital charge of high treason. A few days later two King's Messengers arrived in Norwich with a warrant for the arrest of Isaac Saint, innkeeper of The Pelican in St George's Colegate. While one of them took Saint in charge, the other followed Mrs Saint upstairs and found her removing papers from a drawer. He said he had difficulty in forcing the papers from her but he did so and carried them off to London with the prisoner in a post-chaise. Next morning Saint was interrogated by the Privy Council. The unfortunate innkeeper was faced by the Lord Chancellor, two Dukes, four other lords, Mr Secretary Dundas and the Attorney and Solicitor General. He said that several clubs met in Norwich inns. He had been offered one and had

taken it in. They had proposed to come once a fortnight or
once a month. They employed themselves in reading letters
and were well behaved. He heard them read a letter from
Margarot about the time he was sentenced. He thought the
sentiments in the letter not hostile to the law or to His Majesty.
He tried to imply that his association with the club had been
casual and intended to improve his trade but he was forced to
admit that he had been deeply implicated in the proceedings of
the clubs and had even visited village meetings.[25] His testimony
as to the Norwich organisation agreed closely with what
Alderton had reported. The Habeas Corpus Act having been
suspended Saint was detained for some months but apparently
not charged with any offence.

Shortly after this the government obtained a document
which no doubt confirmed them in their view of the wisdom
of their proceedings—a letter from the Sheffield Constitutional
Society to their correspondents in Norwich and elsewhere
offering pike-blades tempered and polished at 1s each for
defence in case they suffered attack by the administration.[26]

May had been a month of attack against the reformers; June
gave opportunity to the supporters of the status quo to demon-
strate in support of their position. The king's birthday was
enthusiastically observed, the mayor and corporation proces-
sing to the cathedral to hear an apposite sermon by the Rev.
John Peele on the text, "Whether is it better for you that all the
sons of Jerrubaal, threescore and ten persons, reign over you
or that one reign over you". The mayor gave an elegant dinner
to a splendid company and remembered at the same time to
order 10s worth of beer for the prisoners in the city gaol.[27]
Then came news of Lord Howe's victory over the French
fleet—the Glorious first of June—and the corporation paid
two guineas to the bell ringers and £2 5s 1d to James Stannard,
the gunner for firing the city's guns.[28] On the Guild day this
month the new mayor, James Hudson, a banking partner of
the Harveys, was sworn and adressed by the Steward on the
need for the utmost vigilance to preserve our most excellent
constitution—he was to follow Windham's politics and become
a consistent orange-and-purple voter. At the Pleasure Gardens
the occasion was marked by representations of the Engagement

and Victory of the Fleet under Lord Howe, the music including God save the King with grand chorus and Rule Britannia.

The proceedings against Saint and the London leaders of the reform movement alarmed the Norwich democrats. Their society was believed to be on the proscribed list and warrants for the arrest of its leaders were daily expected. William Taylor the younger went through the records and affixed his designation of Junior to all the entries where his father's name appeared. So far as its leaders were concerned the Norwich Revolution Society was suffered to expire.[29] On the other side of politics the Castle Corporation Club continued its annual appointment of a mayor and sheriffs. According to the scribe who kept its record book it became the rallying point for good and loyal citizens who had occasion to make a stand against the activity and zeal of the political demagogues, themselves the dupes of chimerical and delusive doctrines of liberty, equality and reform. He tells us that the club made it its duty to assist in promoting to high office in the city corporation men of good sense, education, public and private virtues and loyalty to their King.[30]

The events of May and June set the scene for an even more remarkable development in July when Windham joined the War Cabinet as Secretary at War. This involved him in standing again for election. The Norwich sheriffs received the writ on Tuesday 8 July. The election took place the following Saturday. In Windham's address to the gentlemen, clergy, freemen and freeholders of the city he said he had joined with those from whom he formerly differed but with whom he now had the happiness perfectly to agree. He hoped to serve what appeared not only the cause of his country but of all the civilised world. He was perfectly satisfied that he had never deviated from those principles which first recommended him to their favour. Those who, to quote the *Norfolk Chronicle*,

> thought his political conduct of late, and particularly his juncture with the present administration inconsistent with his former principles and professions and who totally differed from him with respect to the necessity and continuance of the war as inimical to the commercial interests of this kindgom and this city in particular,

were determined to oppose Windham's re-election. They tried Bartlett Gurney and Alderman Ives of Town Close but neither was willing to stand. On the Friday they held a meeting in St Andrew's Hall when, on the proposal of Dr Rigby, it was agreed to nominate James Mingay of Thetford, a whig barrister and county magistrate, as their candidate. A messenger was sent to Thetford to fetch him but he had gone to London. On the assurance of the probability of Mingay's election his brother, a surgeon, was persuaded to come to Norwich to represent him. When he arrived at the city gates on Saturday morning Mingay's supporters unharnessed his horses and the populace drew the coach to party headquarters. The election started at ten that morning with a meeting in the Guildhall when, after reading the writ and the Act against bribery and corruption, the Mayor nominated Windham. Bartlett Gurney then nominated Mingay. While the poll proceeded the radicals carried round the city a loom hung with black cloth and empty shuttles while Windham's supporters exhibited a model guillotine with a female figure suffering under it, labelled "French Liberty".

At the end of the day Windham was declared elected by 1236 votes against 770. In the north ward—Norwich over the water —where the dissenters were most firmly established, Mingay actually polled a majority of 333 votes to 218. In 1790 when he had the support of the radicals Windham had polled 355 votes here against Hobart's 320. A scrutiny of the poll books shews that of those who had voted for Windham in the 1790 election about half followed him in his change of views and about half transferred their votes to Mingay. A number who had voted for Hobart and not Windham now voted for Mingay, perhaps as an expression of opposition to the war. Mingay afterwards wrote that, though flattered, he was in fact ineligible for election, holding an office of profit under the crown.

At noon on the following Monday the victor underwent the traditional chairing ceremony three times round the marketplace. During the chairing he was hit on the head by a stone and jumping from his seat he seized the culprit and committed him to prison. On the second time round Mr P. J. Knights from the elegant window of his shawl warehouse offered him

wine in a silver goblet. Windham accepted it and turning to
the excited multitude, drank to the health of all and the prosperity of the city. When he left for London his supporters drew
his carriage as far as the hospital. Members of the Constitutional Societies to the number of 2000 celebrated Windham's
victory by assembling at Chapel Field and marching to the
Pantheon in Vauxhall Gardens for an entertainment.

Recruiting for the forces proceeded. In September the
Norwich Volunteer Regiment paraded in the market place
and received its colours from the Mayor.

The Norwich publican Isaac Saint, arrested in May, still
remained in custody,[31] his predicament posing a threat of
similar treatment to the rest of the reforming party in the city.
Yet they were determined to shew the flag and as we shall see
some of them that autumn embarked on a political publication,
The Cabinet. Some went to London to attend the trial of Thomas
Hardy for high treason, which opened at the end of October.
Among them was Amelia Alderson. In a letter to Mrs John
Taylor, Amelia gave an account of a visit to the shop of Daniel
Isaac Eaton, the radical bookseller, which illustrates the con-
spiratorial atmosphere in which the Norwich democrats moved
at this time. A genteel-looking young man came into the shop.
"He examined us and we him; and suspicion being the order
of the day, I dared not talk to Mrs Eaton until the stranger was
engaged in conversation. . . ." She then told Mrs Eaton that she
came from the city of sedition, Norwich. The stranger over-
heard and immediately entered into conversation with them.
Seeing that he was intimate with Mrs Eaton, Amelia had no
fear. Finding he came from Scotland she discussed with him
the events of the Edinburgh convention. He in turn criticised
the Norwich choice of Mingay as a candidate. "Why do the
Norwich patriots espouse Mingay? . . . He might be a very
good implement of resentment against Windham, but though
the friend of their necessity, not of their choice." Amelia
agreed with him in this opinion. After he had gone she learned
that he was Mr Sinclair who had been tried for sedition and
acquitted at Edinburgh. Should Hardy and his associates be
condemned the Aldersons were determined to emigrate to
America.[32]

Another Norwich observer at Hardy's trial was Jonathon Davey. Tradition tells that after the verdict he posted home and went straight to the Baptist chapel in St Paul's where Mark Wilks was conducting worship. Seeing him enter the preacher enquired "What news?" "Not guilty," responded Davey, whereupon Wilks called on the congregation to sing the doxology.

The acquittal of Hardy was followed by that of Horne Tooke and then of Thelwall. These verdicts which delighted the radicals disgusted William Windham. In a speech at the opening of Parliament at the end of December he said that some who had favoured the French Revolution at its commencement could not so soon as others detach their affections from a system that had led to massacre and ruin. Societies formed by this party had propagated doctrines most hostile to the interests of the country. Members of these societies had been acquitted by a jury and gentlemen talked of their innocence in a tone of exultation. He wished them the joy of the innocence of an acquitted felon.

REFERENCES

1. Court of Mayoralty Book.
2. *Parliamentary history*, vol. XXX, p. 539.
3. R. H. Mason, *History of Norfolk*, Part III, p. 471.
4. Diary of Mme. D'Arblay, vol. III, p. 464.
5. P.R.O. Report of the Committee of Secrecy, TS 24/1/5.
6. *Norwich Mercury*, 20 April 1793.
7. *Parl. Hist.*, vol. XXX, p. 786.
8. State Trials, vol. XXIV, p. 630.
9. Mrs Baring, *Diary of Wm. Windham*, p. 290.
10. Ibid, p. 291.
11. Ibid, pp. 292–5.
12. Michael Roe, *Inst. of Hist. Research*, vol. XXXI, p. 70.
13. Mason, op. cit., pp. 472–3.
14. J. Kinghorn to Wm. Richards, 4 Dec. 1793.
15. Court of Mayoralty Book.
16. *Norfolk Chronicle*, 30 Nov. 1793.
17. *Norwich Mercury*, 15 March 1794.
18. Court of Mayoralty Book.
19. J. Matchett, *Norfolk and Norwich Vade Mecum*, p. 37.
20. *Norfolk Chronicle*, 12 Feb. 1794.

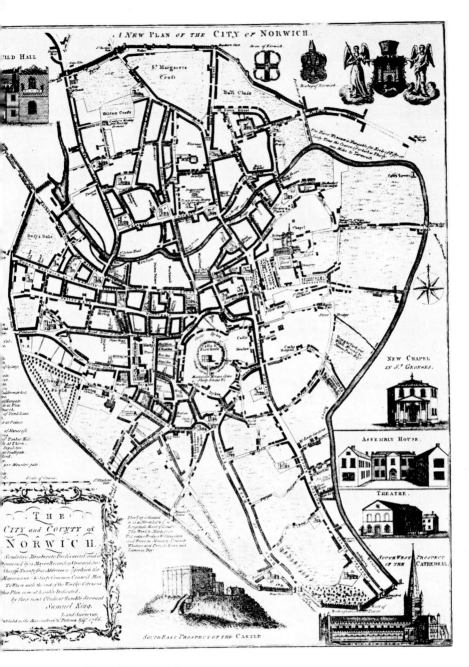

Plate 1   Plan of Norwich in 1766

Plate 2   (Above left) John Harvey in 1803, painting by John Opie

Plate 3   (Above right) John Patteson in about 1800, painting by William Beechey

Plate 4   (Left) Joseph Kinghorn in about 1790, lithograph by J. M. Johnson

21. P.R.O. Treasury Solicitors Papers, TS 24/3/80.
22. State Trials, vol. XXV, p. 229.
23. P.R.O. Report of Committee of Secrecy.
24. *Norwich Mercury*, 12 April 1794.
25. P.R.O. Privy Council papers, PC1/21.
26. P.R.O. Report of Committee of Secrecy.
27. *Norfolk Chronicle* and *Norwich Mercury*, 7 June 1794.
28. Court of Mayoralty Book.
29. J. W. Robberds, *Memoir of Wm. Taylor*, vol. I, p. 75.
30. Castle Corporation Minute Book, N&N Record Office.
31. State Trials, vol. XXIV, 1362.
32. C. L. Brightwell, *Life of Amelia Opie*, p. 45.

5 *The Young Revolutionaries 1793–1795*

In July 1789, before reaching Paris, Dr Rigby and his party, including young Ollyett Woodhouse, an Oxford undergraduate who had entered Pembroke College the year before, passed through Douay, "Where", Rigby recorded, "Master Pitchford is. His college is a very excellent one and Mr Gibson, the president, to whom I had a letter, a polite and sensible man."[1]

Master Pitchford was John, son of a doctor of the same name who, being a Roman Catholic, sent him to be educated in France. Some time before the declaration of war in February 1793 young Pitchford was safe home in Norwich, a devout Christian with a great enthusiasm for the revolution in France. In September 1793 he was acting as secretary of the Tusculan School, a debating society whose members included Ollyett Woodhouse, later to become Advocate General at Bombay, William Firth, a future Steward of Norwich, and Charles Marsh, one day to be a Member of Parliament.

Joseph Kinghorn in a letter to his father dated 22 October wrote:

> I was invited to drink tea &c with a company of young Gentlemen of this city who meet once a week at each other's houses and discuss a proposed question. The question was "Whether Natural Religion was sufficient to lead men to virtue and happiness".

He thought he had been invited to defend the cause of Christianity, several of the gentlemen being professed Deists.

> After tea we got round the table. The Moderator for the evening called to bussiness, read the question and the

debate began. . . . One gentleman at last took up the subject, discussed it a long time, displayed a great deal of first rate ability and wanted to turn everything to the disadvantage of Christianity. To this speech I found it was expected I should reply. . . .

Pitchford, who kept the minutes, noted that Charles Marsh, the previous speaker, in a speech replete with the most splendid oratory, endeavoured to rouse indignation against the crusades and the blood and rapine which had marked the Christian conquest of the new world. "Kinghorne", he recorded, "in a speech of very great length and with great coolness and precision combatted all that Marsh had advanced and lamented that his great talents should be prostituted in the cause of infidelity." On this occasion nine of the young gentlemen voted in favour of the sufficiency of Deism or Natural religion —only five against. Charles Marsh was scarcely 20 at this time; Kinghorn 27. Marsh had entered St John's College, Cambridge in 1792 but he was never to graduate—perhaps his abandonment of the Christian faith precluded it.[2]

Kinghorn was called in again in January 1794 when the question was "Is the intrinsic excellence of pure Christianity a sufficient evidence of its divine original ?" In the course of his speech he remarked that infidels were very ingenious. They made a Christianity of their own and then amused themselves with knocking it down, and, Pitchford noted "Mr K. made a great many more acute and sarcastic remarks on the adversaries of Christianity." This time it was Marsh's turn to reply. He complained that Kinghorn's speech had been full of spleen and devoid of argument. He objected to the pejorative use of the term "infidel". The God of the Infidel, he said, was not the God of Moses or St Paul—what a frightful portrait did they exhibit of the Deity. Persecutions and perplexities had attended the Christian system from its earliest step—it was rotten to the very heart. After this the house was equally divided, five for and five against Christianity. Such was the climate of religious opinion at this time. Catherine Gurney wrote that John Pitchford and Joseph Kinghorn were the only two among the literary young men with whom the Gurneys were acquainted who upheld the cause of religion against the infidelity then prevailing.[3]

The young men of the Tusculan School were even more interested in politics than in religion and their politics had a strong bias towards France and the Revolution. A fortnight after the debate on Natural Religion the question propounded was "Is the constitution of the French Republic superior or inferior to those of Greece or Rome?" This was introduced by Pitchford who, while he regarded the constitution of France as the most perfect that had yet existed, was far from approving their proceedings. He execrated the severity which had familiarised them with blood; he abhorred their contempt for religion; he disapproved their spirit of aggrandisement and conquest. Dr Rigby, a visitor that evening, made a speech vindicating the "égaremens" of the French from their peculiar circumstances. Ollyett Woodhouse tried to contend for the superiority of Sparta from its equality of property, but in the end the society was unanimous in voting the French constitution the best.

In January 1794 they considered whether the measures recently adopted by the government would tend to perpetuate or destroy the present system. This presumably refers to the prosecution of the leaders of the Edinburgh Convention on charges of sedition which had led to sentences of transportation. John Taylor declamed against current abuses and no one was found to disagree with him. Then they debated the question— so familiar in our time—"Are there circumstances that would justify us in refusing to defend our country?" Discussion on this subject continued to a late hour and was remarkable for the contrariety of opinion. In March they were asking "Has the government of a country a right to compell its citizens to arm?" Hudson Gurney made an animated speech against any such right. Pitchford was against it prima facie but was staggered by the advantages of the compulsory requisition by the French republic.

By this time some of the members were becoming alarmed for their own safety. Tom Houghton wanted to exclude the discussion of political subjects as being dangerous but his motion was not seconded. Politics was so much in their minds that any subject was likely to lead to political discussion. On 28 March the question was "Has not the knowledge of letters been the chief source of human misery?" This provoked Pitchford, in opposition, to cite the glorious effects produced by science in France: the beautiful spectacle of a whole people gradually enlightened, at length with one common effort bursting the bands of despotism. Again in April they debated whether political subjects ought to be discussed in literary societies at such a time. Once more Houghton contended that such discussion was fruitless and dangerous. Persons in much the same predicament, he said, had been sentenced to fourteen years transportation. He looked with dread at a period when members of the Tusculan School might share the same fate. Pitchford said they agreed in the grand principles of general liberty but differed in detail, e.g. on the superiority of the American or the French constitutions, of the Gironde or Mountain party. From the collision of these opinions truth should result. He undertook not to insert anything treasonable in the Tusculanum. Hudson Gurney thought that with one party rushing into despotism it was their serious duty to communicate their sentiments. France had nearly been ruined by conspiracies; how were the villians who endeavoured to strangle the infant liberty detected and brought to punishment but by the continual discussions of popular societies? Personal danger was no sufficient reason to deter men professing themselves friends of truth. Of the six present no one else supported Houghton. When they met again on 11 April Houghton introduced the question, "Anne libertas unquam quam sub rege pio gratior extat?" Someone pointed to the despotism of the convention in France, the rapid succession of characters, splendid beginnings and bloody exits of the ephemeral governors of that unhappy country. Charles Marsh defended the French. Surrounded as they were by the most formidable combination of foreign enemies and distracted by internal plots, a system of rigid coercion was necessary to the very existence of the Republic. Only Houghton and one other favoured monarchy. The next meeting voted by a small majority that the 1688 Revolution did not merit the appelation "Glorious". Two more sessions on 25 May and 2 April discussed the propriety of civil government instituting laws against irreligious opinions. At this point the record stops. Either the society ceased to meet or it was thought prudent no longer to keep records. As we have seen this was the month when the leaders of the London societies were arrested, Isaac Saint carried off and the Habeas Corpus Act suspended.

Next autumn, however, the young men who had formed the Tusculan School involved themselves in a new and scarcely less hazardous venture, publishing *The Cabinet*, comprising original pieces on topics connected with the science of civil polity, law, and the constitution at the price of 6d.

> No work in the English language, perhaps, ever appeared . . . under circumstances more inauspicious and depressing than the Cabinet. . . . The public mind, seduced by the base artifices of a designing and profligate adminis-tration, rejected with a furious disdain every attempt at rational reform.
>
> The French revolution . . . still seemed to promise the sublime spectacle of a great and powerful nation governing itself on the principles of liberty and equality; and although a too sudden transition from abject slavery to . . . perfect liberty had produced many crimes . . . yet the change seemed likely to be ultimately productive of much good.
>
> The nation itself had been frightened . . . by the insti-tution of a system of TERROR almost as hideous in its features, almost as gigantic in its stature, And infinitely more pernicious in its tendency than France ever knew.

So the "Society of Gentlemen" who originated *The Cabinet* saw their situation when they first went to press in September 1794. Their apprehension of an English terror may seem to us grossly exaggerated but at the time the trials of Hardy, Thelwall and others on capital charges were pending and the gentlemen of the society had reason to fear that any day warrants might be served on themselves. Yet they were not deterred. Their object, they said, was to remind their fellow citizens of their duties and their rights. To render the illustration of political principles more palatable they included a proportion of "literature", excluding only theology and metaphysics. The contributions to *The Cabinet* were anonymous save for a series of code signs at the foot of each article. The bound copy preserved in the Norfolk and Norwich Library has on its fly sheet a manuscript key to some of the codes from which the greater part of the series may be attributed. Charles Marsh acted as editor and contributed a number of articles on emigration, holding that departure to America was a gross violation of the duty to stay and check the precipitate degeneracy of the age. He also wrote on the connection of the arts and sciences with Liberty, echoing the Tusculan debates. Some years later, after being called to the Bar, Marsh was himself to emigrate to India. He practised successfully at Madras and later returned to enter Parliament as member for East Retford. John Pitchford was the largest contributor, writing a long series on the history of the war and waxing eloquent on its deplorable effects. He also wrote on the unequal division of property, lamenting the lot of the day labourer with his toilsome fourteen-hour day and the weaver working all the daylight hours. His views were supported in an article by Dr Rigby who considered the melancholy state of the lower orders proof of the imperfection of the present organisation of society. In America, he said, conditions were much better, the average price of labour being 3s a day and necessaries about half their cost in England.

Thomas Starling Norgate, aged 22, son of the alderman, was another large contributor. He wrote on the cultivation of waste lands, arguing that enclosure was beneficial to the poor even under the present unsatisfactory system of distribution. He wrote on the rights of women, who, he thought, should be represented in parliament; and on the diffusion of knowledge, opining that given a wider spread of political knowledge the people would not suffer themselves to be led to the slaughter in the field of battle. T. S. Norgate was later to become a pillar of the establishment and founder of the Norfolk and Norwich Horticultural Society. Among other contributors Amelia Alderson was 25 years old, William Taylor 29. They had the support of several of the older generation—Dr Rigby, John Taylor, Dr Enfield and the Rev. Thomas Drummond, but the bulk of the work was that of the young.

It must be confessed that *The Cabinet* is dull stuff. Though

strongly anti-government it did not contain much that could
have been taken as evidence against its writers. Though pro-
French it had a good deal to say about French errors and
excesses. It was strongly anti-war. Marsh attributed the war
to the machinations of the émigrés and enlarged on the deplorable effects of it. One writer noted as a fact that whoever
spoke in favour of reform was branded a Jacobin. While this
was no doubt true it is hard to imagine anyone taking strong
exception to Dr Enfield's view of the need of such temperate
reform as, without hazarding the peace of society, would lead
to a more equitable diffusion of personal comfort and social
enjoyment.

After the failure of the treason trials *The Cabinet* writers
became a little more forthright in their expressions. They even
discussed the necessity of a convention of the people—that
bugbear of the government—with the object of re-establishing
peace by demonstrating to Parliament the will of the people.
The most violent words in the whole series are in the unat-
tributed Ode to Moderation;

> Thine is the shield the bloodiest tyrants bear
> Foul harbinger of death, black herald of despair
> . . . .
>
> O rather bear me fury, vengeance wild!
> To the red scene of slaughter and dismay,
> Where the bold multitude, no more beguiled
> The dreadful banners of their rage display.

The Cabinet was not likely to appeal to the uneducated and
illiterate, a fact that rendered it relatively harmless from the
point of view of the government. Its writers were no doubt in
touch with the Blue and White party in the city. In January
1795, when a meeting of citizens in St Andrew's Hall petitioned
for the ending of hostilities, *The Cabinet* carried an article on the
alarming situation in the country calling for petitions to remove
those ministers who by crimes and incapacity have lost our
confidence and to entreat the Father of his People to make
immediate peace with the victorious Republic of France.

After publishing for twelve months it was judged wise to

discontinue *The Cabinet*. Amelia Alderson who had written an
ode on the theme:

> Gallia shall bid the world be free
> And war his blood-stained throne resign. . . .

besides contributing a number of romantic and sentimental
verses, wrote: "What a pity it is that The Cabinet is dangerous.
I should have enjoyed it else so much."

REFERENCES

1. Lady Eastlake, op. cit., p. 14.
2. This and all further references to the Tusculan Society are from
   the "Tusculanum" in the N&N Record Office.
3. A. J. C. Hare, *Gurneys of Earlham*, vol. I, p. 83.

6 Norwich Politics 1795–1796

At the opening of 1795 the price of wheat and consequently that of bread was increasing; employment was scarce and the city war-weary. Instead of raising the poor rate a subscription was opened to supplement relief. The city's Members of Parliament subscribed £50 each, the Dean and Chapter a similar amount. The manager of the Theatre Royal gave £30, the proceeds of a Saturday night's entertainment. Some collectors met with the objection that the distress was due to the war and unless the cause were removed subscriptions might do more harm than good but John Gurney and Dr Lubbock, both supporters of the anti-war party, combatted this view, pointing out that the distresses of the poor were apparent and pressing.[1] The corporation held a special assembly and sent a petition to the King beseeching His Majesty to use every means he might judge expedient to terminate the present calamitious and destructive war which had nearly annihilated the manufactures and trade of this once flourishing city and reduced the majority of its inhabitants—the industrious poor—to a state of extreme distress.[2] A meeting of citizens was called to St Andrews Hall on 28 January to send a similar petition to Parliament. Upwards of a thousand people were present. The mayor, James Hudson opened the business, Bartlett Gurney moved the petition and it was seconded by Sigismund Trafford, a man of means and an enthusiastic radical. Trafford's grandfather, Clement Boehm, a Strasbourg merchant, had settled in London and become a director of the Bank of England. The grandson acquired estates at Wroxham a few miles from Norwich and assumed the name of Trafford. The petition emphasised the distresses of the lower classes, reduced to a state of misery never before experienced, and prayed that by renouncing all interference in the internal affairs of France and by such measures as they deemed expedient, they should endeavour a speedy peace. A slight attempt in the meeting to "provoke a political discussion" was soon squashed. The petition was signed by the mayor, though a tory, and by over 5500 citizens on a scroll 99 feet long.[3] When Henry Hobart presented the petition to the Commons, Thomas William Coke twitted him on not giving it the importance it deserved. The petition, Coke maintained, spoke the unanimous sense of the opulent city of Norwich. People who had been deluded into war were now convinced of its ruinous consequences. Some signing the petition had been warm supporters of William Windham and the war. They had seen their error.[4] Coke considered that he had first hand knowledge of Norwich opinion for he was wont to come up to the city on market days and to visit the John Taylors' house in St George's Colegate where whig enthusiasts foregathered to talk politics with Mrs Taylor as she sat by the fire darning her children's stockings.[5] Hobart agreed that the people of Norwich had suffered and the petition spoke their sentiments. Just then Norwich had additional troubles. The same papers which reported the presentation of the petition recorded another disaster. A rapid thaw caused the river to rise till the water was higher than the arch of St Miles' bridge and inundated the lower parts of the city so that people could only leave their houses by boat or on horseback. A house near Duke's Palace yard was washed away. Yet another subscription list had to be opened to help the unfortunate.

The anti-war tide flowing so freely in Norwich did not reach to the neighbouring town of Yarmouth. That February the corporation there sent an address to the King promising a cheerful contribution to the present just and necessary war. But Yarmouth and Norwich still had interests in common for we find the Norwich Court of the Mayoralty in March 1795 sending a memorial to the Privy Council asking them to lift the embargo on London and Hull traders visiting Yarmouth as otherwise they fear the public will suffer great inconvenience from want of cheese, groceries, and other articles.[6]

Feeling perhaps that he could rely on widespread support from his fellow citizens in their present mood, Mark Wilks advertised his intention to preach two collection sermons in St Paul's chapel towards defraying the expenses of the defence in the recent high treason trials. He took his text from the words of Athaliah in II Kings XL, 14, "Treason, Treason". The vilest characters, he said, are sometimes the first to accuse and the worst of crimes are sometimes imputed to the best of men. As to the local scene:

> The jacobins in this city, and except those at Paris there can have been none greater, have given repeated demonstrations of their love of peace. At a time when the starving poor felt an iniquitous disposition to riot . . . the affiliated societies in this city published this resolve: "That if any member should break the peace, by violation of the existing laws, he should not only be excluded but delivered up into the hands of justice".

Ridiculing the attitude of the government Wilks told that when the friends of freedom met to celebrate the deliverance of the "acquitted felons" the Duke of Portland sent orders to the mayor to parade the streets with constables to preserve the peace and that the mayor replied vindicating the injured character of his fellow-citizens. Of the state of the poor Wilks painted a gloomy picture:

> . . . their tattered rags, naked limbs, useless looms, strawless beds, sparkless hearths, with their ghastly looks and the unavailing cries of their helpless infants . . .

It was not surprising that, despite the resolve of the affiliated societies, such conditions should lead to incipient rioting on the market. On 3 May the magistrates ordered a handbill to be printed assuring all persons coming to the market with provisions that every care would be taken to protect them and their property and to punish with the utmost severity any riotous conduct.[7] Rioting was quelled but conditions got worse and the price of bread dearer though it was said that Norwich bakers gave better weight than the law required.[8] In July the mayor besought the government to direct six cargoes of wheat to Norwich. The city magistrates and the members of the grand jury agreed to use only wholemeal bread in their families and ten firms of millers at a meeting in the city agreed not to send any wheat or flour out of the country during the present scarcity.[9] The voice of the poor was heard in an anonymous letter printed in Norwich, dated 21 July, addressed "Perishing Citizens", complaining of those who waste the finest wheat on their worthless heads—an allusion to the use of flour for hairdressing—and who are promising French rebels supplies, thus transporting to traitors articles that should feed citizens.

> O Countrymen! were you but wise, could you distinguish between your country's enemies and her truest friends! were you but acquainted with your own dignity, power, and importance in the social world; were you once determined legally to correct the errors of state delinquents, you would not be reduced to the dire necessity of eating Bran; your tables would be furnished with the bounties of Providence; and the guilty authors of your distress would be sent to Germany to eat straw.[10]

The author of this letter was evidently acquainted with The Rights of Man in which Paine recounts an anecdote of a soldier from Brunswick who said, "In my country if the prince says Eat Straw, we eat straw".

In October the weekly allowance for boys in the Boy's Hospital which had stood at 3s 6d a head since 1791 had to be raised by 1s "till a reduction in the price of provisions". The court of the mayoralty once more directed a memorial to the city Members of Parliament on the dearness and scarcity of provisions, calling on them to bring forward and support measures calculated to reduce the exorbitant prices of the necessaries of life and to attain for the country the dignity, prosperity and true glory to be looked for in the restoration of peace.[11] The wording of the resolution had been designed with great care to satisfy the tory majority who held that the timing of peace negotiations must be left to the government and the whig members who thought they should be entered upon at once. Its nuances were not appreciated by the Norwich newspapers who reported the last phrase as ". . . true glory which can only be acquired by the Restoration of Peace", a too whiggish version for which the printers were reprimanded by the court.

For almost a year after the arrest of Isaac Saint there is no evidence of activity of the radical clubs in Norwich. But no doubt the men who had formed them continued to frequent their habitual ale houses so that the reconstitution of organised activity would not be difficult. So in April 1795 the Norwich Patriotic Society was established with the same objectives as the former Revolution Society. Its manifesto declared that the great end of civil society was general happiness; that every individual (minors, criminals and the insane excepted) had a right to share in the government to whose support he contributed, either in person or by representation; that annually elected parliaments would be consistent with the principles of the British constitution; that in consequence of unequal representation, corruption, oppressive taxes, and unjust laws, restrictions of liberty and waste of public money had ensued. The Patriots expressed their abhorrence of tumult and violence, aimed at reform not anarchy and proposed to employ reason, firmness and unanimity to persuade their fellow citizens. The members were to meet fortnightly in divisions of 30 and to pay a minimum subscription of one penny at each meeting.[12] That September John Lightbody, secretary of the society, informed a correspondent that numbers were increasing fast and that at the next meeting they would have 27 divisions. In November they intended to celebrate the anniversary of the acquittal of citizen Hardy with a public dinner at The Rose. As they understood that the "Loyal Clubs" were going to petition parliament on the high price of grain they had decided not to meddle in the matter.[13] It appears that the Patriotic Society actually secured the presence of Hardy for their celebrations. A sarcastic notice appeared in the *Norwich Mercury* of 21 November purporting to express the thanks of the shopkeepers, tradesmen, journeymen and working poor to the Jacobin societies for their polite invitation to citizen Hardy and for the sumptuous entertainments (notwithstanding the high price of provisions) provided during his abode here.

The population was by no means unanimous in supporting the reforming and anti-war line. Doubtless in some cases the very scarcity was an aid to recruiting for the armed forces at least offered food, clothing and a job. The view that the war must be prosecuted to victory received official support at various festivals during the year. In May in honour of the queen's birthday the United Constitutional Societies* processed through the city with a beautiful boy on horseback representing the genius of Britain, supported by a soldier and a sailor. The procession terminated at Keymer's Pantheon where 3000 people assembled.[14] Next month to celebrate the king's birthday the mayor and corporation went in procession to the cathedral, whereafter the Queen's Bays and three regiments lately returned from the continent fired vollies in the market place. They then marched to Coe's gardens where they sat down with their wives and children to a repast of 570 dishes of roast, boiled and baked meats, 600 3d loaves and 14 barrels of porter (for which repast 100 guineas had been subscribed). After this entertainment they returned to barracks with bands playing.[15]

Unofficially troops stationed here took part in the life of the city in other ways. Writing to Joseph Kinghorn on holiday in Yorkshire, Thomas Hawkins who was responsible for filling his pulpit:

> I have been called upon to exercise my opinion on the propriety of admitting a Red Coat Parson to your pulpit. A Sergeant in the Warwick Militia whose name is Burton have been preaching at the Tabernacle and at Newton's [Old Meeting] with great popularity and some of our people were much surprised I did not ask him to fill the pulpit on Sabbath day afternoons at St Mary's. . . . Altho' I have no doubt the Sergeant is a good man, yet after hearing him twice I did not think him calculated to instruct a regular Dissenting congregation. . . .

When the King went to open Parliament at the end of October he was hooted by the mob. Woodforde, who was passing through London, witnessed the incident and wrote

> His Majesty was very grossly insulted by some of the Mob, and had a very narrow escape of being killed going to the House, a ball passing thro' the windows as he went thro' Old Palace Yard.

* In the kaleidoscope of the times the term "United Constitutional Societies" in 1795 appears to have acquired the opposite political connotation from the same term as used by the radicals a year before (see p. 46).

Francis Place, a member of the London Corresponding Society gave a rather different account of the incident:

> On October 29 [1795] the King went to open Parliament An immense number of people had assembled in St James's Park who hissed and groaned and continually called out—No Pitt, no War, Bread, Bread, Peace, Peace.
>
> When the coach had nearly reached the House of Peers one of the windows was Broken—this happened in the narrow street between St Margarets & Henry VII Chapel —A pretence was set up that the King had been shot at & an inference drawn of a plot to kill him.[16]

The government at once took occasion to introduce two Bills, one making it a treasonable offence to incite the people by speech to hatred or contempt of the king, constitution or government; the other forbidding meetings of over 50 persons without prior notice to a magistrate, defiance of whose orders was to be punishable by death. These Bills were universally unpopular.

The Norwich court of the mayoralty sent a rather curiously worded address to the king. After congratulating him on his escape and assuring him of their endeavours to promote obedience to the law, they said:

> We gratefully rely on Your Majesty's paternal solicitude for your People's welfare and on the wisdom of the legislature to adopt such speedy and salutary measures as may tend to alleviate the distresses of the poor and promote the negotiation of an honourable peace and concilliate national prosperity with constitutional security.[17]

Meanwhile a Common Hall was called to raise a petition against the two bills. Sigismund Trafford was in the chair and Mark Wilks proposed the resolution. Wilks enlarged upon the danger of making the monarch an object of terror.

> . . . Such is the philanthropy of our gracious sovereign, such the mildness of his disposition and the goodness of his heart, it would be no easy task to make him a tyrant but should the . . . legislature frame tyrannic laws and

Plate 5 (Above left) Dr Edward Rigby in 1815, engraving by Mrs Dawson Turner

Plate 6 (Above right) John Cozens in about 1800, by kind permission of John Copeman & Sons Ltd

Plate 7 (Right) Hudson Gurney in 1797, engraving by John Opie

Plate 8   Interior of the Octagon Chapel

Plate 9   View of Gurney's Bank, taken from London Lane

prevail on him to give reluctantly his royal assent and signature, it is to be dreaded they would, by that act, sign and seal his death warrent, build his sepulchre and toll his passing bell.

Alderman Robert Harvey argued against a petition and was heard with respectful silence though Wilks took exception to his intervention on the grounds that should the Bills become law he as a magistrate might be called upon to implement them. Trafford and Ollyett Woodhouse then read the petition from different parts of the hustings and it was agreed by acclamation. The petitioners, it said, viewed the two Bills with extreme surprise and great alarm as infringements of the constitution. They lamented the late insult to the king but thought existing laws adequate to deal with it. They considered that to deprive the people of the means of complaining would drive them to measures the petitioners would deprecate.[18] Eventually the petition with 5000 signatures was sent to Charles James Fox and presented to the House. A week later an address was presented to His Majesty from the gentlemen, clergy, merchants and inhabitants of Norwich deploring the wild and destructive theories which have caused crimes and miseries in a neighbouring country and confiding in the wisdom and integrity of Parliament for such wise and temperate restraints as might be necessary to restore the situation at home.[19]

Not long after this one of Wilks's friends picked up in the street a letter from Windham to his Norwich agent, the text of which was published by the radicals by way of propaganda. The letter, dated 21 November 1795, included this paragraph:

One of my present objects in writing is to enquire about a fact I have heard repeated from the late meeting for the purpose of a petition against the two Bills now depending, viz. that Mark Wilks declared that "if the King consenteth to these bills, he would not live a month". If this be true I wish you would endeavour to get evidence of it in order that it may be considered what it may be proper to do upon it. If there is any doubt of the expressions, it would be best that no notice should be taken and at all events that any enquiry should be conducted in a manner not to

F

excite any alarm or give them reason to suppose that it was made by any suggestion from here.[20]

Wilks's daughter tells us that the discovery of this letter made him more vigilant and cautious. Already another Baptist minister, William Winterbotham, had been sent to prison for two political sermons he had preached at Plymouth, though his conviction seems to have been due to the perversity of the jury in the face of the judge's summing up.

The Norwich Patriotic Society wrote to the London Corresponding Society on 14 December that they had been fully engaged in conducting opposition. If nothing could prevent the Bills passing, they asked what London proposed as its future line of conduct. They themselves were determined by all legal and constitutional means to procure their object of a radical reform of Parliament.[21]

In December the price of bread reached its highest yet. The court of the mayoralty agreed to make another effort to reduce the consumption of wheat in their own families. Besides using only wholemeal bread they would forego the use of wheaten flour in pastry and diminish its use so far as possible for anything else. They recommended the same practice to their fellow citizens. Several journeymen-hotpressers were foolish enough to try to mend their situation by a demand for higher wages and were convicted of entering into an unlawful combination. A notice was issued reminding citizens that the penalty for this offence was three months hard labour in the house of correction.[22] The mace officers whose duty was to attend upon the mayor were more successful. Their salary was £8 per annum plus 1s 6½d for every ale house licence. They complained that the number of licences had decreased and it was difficult for them to keep up appearances. The corporation allowed them an increase to £12.[23]

Despite all efforts at economy wheat became scarcer. After a further price rise in April 1796 a number of exasperated poor followed Mr Bloom, the Trowse miller, with shrieks and groans to the marketplace. Mr Bloom took refuge in the Guildhall whereupon the crowd tried to break down the door. A sergeant's guard of the Inniskillings was sent for from the barracks who escorted Bloom safely away through a shower of sticks, stones and potatoes. A few days later a mob attacked baker's shops in St Mary's and St Martin's. The magistrates decided to call for the help of the citizens rather than the military. The mayor and sheriffs with a posse of supporters proceeded to the places where disorder was rife. The Riot Act was read. Three rioters who refused to depart quietly were arrested.[24] Arrangements were made in case of future rioting to summon the citizens by ringing St Peter's bells and 300 quarter-staves were ordered to be kept at the Guildhall for use in preserving the peace.[25] To alleviate the current distress the mayor and twelve of the aldermen subscribed £100 each to buy meal and flour to be retailed cheaply under the direction of a committee.[26]

In May came the excitement of a General Election. The sheriffs received the writ on Saturday 21 May. On the same day Windham's address to the electors appeared in the papers. To those who looked with complacency to the final establishment of the French system in that country and who could hardly fail to look for the introduction of some portion of it here, he wrote, he could have no claim to favour. He was sure that such was not the prevailing sentiment in the city. During the campaign the Patriotic Society was lampooned in a handbill purporting to be signed by "Citizen Lighthead, Secretary" and others not so easily identifiable, advertising for an enterprising man to become candidate. He must be willing to give up the glorious constitution founded by our ancestors for that wild chaos of anarchy, confusion, murder and rebellion beautifully exhibited by the French Republic. He must be a perfect master of the guillotine to lop off the heads of opponents and should occasion require be qualified to take off his own.

The election was fixed for Wednesday 25 May. On the Monday the tories held a meeting at the White Swan with William Herring, the mayor-elect, in the chair, at which the sitting members, Henry Hobart and William Windham, were nominated. The same afternoon the opposition party held a meeting at St Andrew's Hall and nominated Bartlett Gurney. Their candidate was away in the north country but his kinsman Joseph Gurney produced a letter agreeing, should he be elected, to represent those who were heartily tired of the war and the present ruinous administration. The radicals were in a confident mood having that spring for the first time secured a majority of supporters on the common council of the city. They procured John Thelwall, hero of the treason trials, to support their cause.

Thomas Hawkins wrote to Joseph Kinghorn, then in Yorkshire:

> We have got Thelwall. He have begun to Lecture. I am going to hear him this evening. He is to give us a digression on the constitution and fate of Poland. I heard him last Evening from the Leads over Cozen's Shop. [The shop was on Gentlemen's Walk and the leads over its bow windows would provide a convenient pulpit for addressing an assembly on the marketplace.] He is a most powerful speaker. I suppose between 4 and 5000 people heard every word distinctly and he gave Windham a most severe trimming. Every sentence bore hard on his antagonist and he gave the people a good view of their own consequence.

Parson Woodforde was kept informed of the progress of the election and supposed Windham would succeed although "very unpopular at present at Norwich amongst the Revolutionists and which are great numbers at Norwich especially Dissenters."

On the day of the poll neither Windham nor Gurney were present. There was considerable disorder and violence. The *Norfolk Chronicle* says that for three hours parties of desperadoes attacked anyone who had the courage to display Windham's colours. On the other side Thelwall complained that he was assaulted in the hall and twice knocked down. The whig report alleged that Gurney's resolution not to procure votes by threats, promises or rewards was strictly adhered to. At the end of the day the votes were:

Hobart 1622   Windham 1159   Gurney 1076.

The radicals were quick to point out that Gurney in fact had a majority over Windham in the votes of Norwich residents. It was the 328 "out-votes" that gave the War Minister his seat. Gurney had mustered only 123 votes from away. Louisa Gurney, aged eleven, recorded in her journal how she watched the election from "Friend Toll's" shop in the market place, adorned with a blue cockade and bawling "Gurney for ever". When she heard that Windham had got the election—"I was so vexed—Eliza and I cried. I hated all aristocrats: I felt it right to hate them. I was fit to kill them."[27]

That June Peter Willsea, a plumber and glazier, was chosen president of the Patriotic Society in succession to Richard Dinmore a sadler. The society collected £13 towards the defence of two reformers on trial at Warwick. In September they reported to London that the treasurer of their society (Jonathon Davey) had been put up for election as sheriff but lost by a small majority. (Actually he polled 189 votes against 386.) The successful candidate (Edmund Reeve) though not a member of their society was a friend to it.[28] In fact Reeve who was a grocer was a consistent blue and white voter. After several attempts Davey was to be elected sheriff in 1800.

Meanwhile the constant pressure of the reformers in Norwich and elsewhere coupled with the demand of financial interests in London for peace were taking effect. Pitt persuaded the King that it was necessary to open negotiations and that only when the French had refused to conclude a reasonable peace would the opponents of hostilities be induced to support the war effort. Accordingly Lord Malmesbury was sent to Paris in October, "Travelling," wrote the infuriated Burke, "the whole way on his knees".

At the same time Pitt was taking less popular steps to protect the country from invasion. An Act was passed to raise a supplementary militia and to add 15,000 seamen to the fleet by a compulsory quota on all parishes. When the Lord Lieutenant tried to hold a meeting in Norwich to implement the Act interruptions by "a few ill informed and misguided persons" compelled him to adjourn it. When the meeting was reconvened a crowd paraded the streets carrying effigies of Pitt, Windham and Dr Horsley, Bishop of Rochester, an outspoken opponent of the Revolution, which they afterwards burned on Mousehold heath.[29] The parish overseers who were charged with the business of finding recruits, were slow to move. When the day appointed for making their returns had come and gone the majority of them were still dragging their feet. The overseers

of 28 Norwich parishes were summoned before the justices
who said they were satisfied that the default was not due to
wilful neglect or disobedience and gave them a further fourteen
days to complete their task. Despite the shew of opposition
Lord Townshend caused the regimentals for the Norfolk
Supplementary Militia to be made up in the city from Norwich
cloth.[30]

Supporters of the government published a notice addressed
to the Loyal and Constitutional Societies inviting public-
spirited persons to come forward as volunteers and pointing
out that a safe and permanent peace might be frustrated by
those who divided the people and formented the public against
defence measures.[31]

As Pitt had expected Malmesbury's negotiations had little
effect on the French. They were not disposed to reason and on
16 December, having dispatched a fleet to invade Ireland, they
ordered him home.

"Bad news indeed," wrote Parson Woodforde, "The French
in short are afraid of making Peace, for fear of the Consequences
which might arise from dismembering their great Armies."

REFERENCES

 1. *Norfolk Chronicle*, 10 Jan. 1795.
 2. Norwich Assembly Book.
 3. *Norwich Chronicle*, 31 Jan., 7 Feb. 1795.
 4. *Norfolk Chronicle*, 14 Feb. 1795.
 5. Janet Ross, *Three Generations of Englishwomen*, p. 25.
 6. Court of Mayoralty Book.
 7. Court of Mayoralty Book.
 8. *Norwich Mercury*, 18 July 1795.
 9. *Norfolk Chronicle*, 18 July 1795.
10. Public Record Office, TS 25/3/81.
11. Court of Mayoralty Book.
12. Declaration of Norwich Patriotic Society. Nch. Local History
    Library.
13. R. W. Ketton-Cremer, *Forty Norfolk Essays*, p. 72.
14. *Norfolk Chronicle*, 23 May 1795.
15. *Norfolk Chronicle*, 6 June 1795.
16. Mary Thrale, *Autobiography of Francis Place*, p. 146.
17. Court of Mayoralty Book.
18. Proceedings and Speeches at the Meeting 17 Nov. 1795.
    Norwich Local History Library.

19. *Norwich Mercury*, 28 Nov. 1795.
20. Norfolk & Norwich Parliamentary Addresses. Norwich Local History Library.
21. Public Record Office, P/C 3107.
22. *Norwich Mercury*, 9 Jan. 1796.
23. Assembly Book.
24. *Norfolk Chronicle*, 30 April 1796.
25. Court of Mayoralty Book.
26. *Norfolk Chronicle*, 30 April 1796.
27. A. J. C. Hare, *The Gurneys of Earlham*, vol. I, p. 53.
28. British Museum, 27815 L.C.S. letter book.
29. *Norwich Mercury*, 19, 26 Nov. 1796.
30. *Norwich Mercury*, 14 Jan. 1797.
31. *Norwich Mercury*, 10 Dec. 1796.

7 *Norwich Politics 1797–1799*

Although the victories of the French on the continent posed a threat to Britain, sympathisers with the Revolution could still admire French successes. Amelia Alderson visiting London where she enjoyed high society and made friends with aristocratic French émigrés wrote to Mrs John Taylor:

> . . . I heard H. Tooke and Fox speak, and that's something. To be sure I had rather have heard Buonaparte address his soldiers; but as pleasure delayed is not pleasure lost, I may still hope to hear him when the bonnet rouge has taken the place of the tiara. . . . But alas! this is no laughing matter,—or rather let us laugh while we can, for I believe an hour to be approaching when salut et fraternité will be the watchwords for civil slaughter throughout Europe; and the meridian glory of the sun of Liberty in France will light us to courting the past dangers and horrors of the republic, in the hopes of obtaining her present power and greatness.

She foresaw with horror the probability of friends equally dear to her meeting one another in mortal combat.[1] She seems to have felt this to be ordained by fate. Others took a more practical view of the situation and began to see the necessity of preparing themselves for the defence of their homeland. As the *Norfolk Chronicle* said:

> To defend our country against the common enemy is now the only measure left to us and no man, whatever his political opinions, will hesitate to take his share of danger and fatigue.[2]

There was also the motive that volunteers might make better terms for themselves than pressed men. In February 1797 a numerous meeting at the Castle Inn with John Patteson in the chair resolved to form a corps of infantry to be called The Norwich Loyal Military Association. They would learn the use of arms and serve without pay while resident in the city. They would aid the civil magistrate but would not undertake to be marched out of the city. The commissioned officers were to be chosen by the subscribers. The city would be asked for the use of St Andrew's Hall for exercises and the government to supply arms. The Loyal Military Association achieved official recognition and in March the city chamberlain was authorised to issue a musket and bayonet to each of its members.[3] When the War Office list was published the names of John Patteson and nine other officers were included. About the same time The Norwich Light Horse Volunteers were formed with John Harvey as captain. They were constituted on similar principles but declared their willingness to march out of Norfolk if required in case of invasion. They appealed to the commanding officer at the cavalry barracks to direct a proper person for their training. Each gentleman was to get his horse properly trained and to be instructed in the exercise of the Hungarian broadsword. Their uniform was a dark blue coat with black velvet collar and cuffs and uniform buttons, military boots, white breeches, helmet, black stock and rosette.[4] For some reason there was a delay in the recognition of the Light Horse Volunteers. Robert Harvey junior wrote to Windham in March that he was seriously chagrined by the check and discouragement this gave to the augmentation of the troup—at present numbering 26, each at the expense of £12 in his equipment.[5]

French triumphs had other less satisfactory effects. People began to withdraw their bank balances for more primitive forms of hoarding. On 26 February the King made a proclamation authorising the suspension of cash payments. The Norwich Court of Mayoralty met two days later and issued a statement on the situation. The scarcity of specie, they said, appeared to have arisen from ill-founded and exaggerated alarms. They recommended the citizens not to withdraw specie from usual circulation. Norwich banks were entitled to the greatest credit and confidence. The affluent situation of the parties concerned in them precluded every doubt as to the security of the notes issued by them.[6]

The Bank of England was now empowered to issue £1 and £2 notes. Woodforde tells us they reached Norwich on 8 March and "the dissaffected to the Government very mad at it". Kinghorn wrote that everybody was afraid of the paper, farmers especially. Despite this the new note issue was a great success and was to remain in force for nearly a quarter of a century.

Meanwhile there had been a new gleam of hope. On 4 March news reached the city of the victory over the Spanish fleet at Cape St Vincent. This battle had an additional interest from the prominent part played by Captain Berry, who had family connections in Norwich and was shortly to marry his cousin Louisa, daughter of the Rev. Samuel Forster, master of the Grammar School. When Nelson boarded the San Nicholas he found Berry already in possession of the poop. He then boarded the larger ship, San Josef, which had drifted against the San Nicholas and there received the surrender of the swords of the officers of the two ships, one of which he subsequently presented to the city of Norwich. It remains to this day in the old Council Chamber of the Guildhall, a permanent memento of the victory. At the time we are told this victory dispelled the general gloom arising from the pecuniary measures. Nothing was now to be heard except expressions of congratulation and the ringing and firing of bells.[7]

In April 1797 loyalists received further encouragement from the visit to the city of Prince William Frederick in his military capacity of Major General. He was billeted at the King's Head, no doubt occupying the best chamber which Woodforde described some years before—"very fine white Dimity Furniture, very full and fringed". No sooner was his arrival reported than the Mayor, Steward, Alderman and Sheriffs crossed the market place to bid him welcome. Although only 21, the prince had already distinguished himself in the fighting in Flanders. He seems to have entered into Norwich affairs with commendable enthusiasm. He visited the Cathedral, Bishop's Palace, public halls and library. He went to the Norfolk and Norwich Hospital and to the Castle where he found a convict, Robert Scott, awaiting the gallows. He made an application on Scott's behalf but was not successful. Alderman Patteson shewed him his brewery and explained to him the working of the Norwich manufactury of stuffs. He met Mr Knights whose Shawl Warehouse adjoined the King's Head and arranged for him to call on his mother, the Duchess of Gloucester, from whom in due course he received an order for a "shawl bed".

The prince entered into the social life of the city. He attended the theatre and patronised the Assembly at Chapel Field House at which tickets were available to all who could afford them—gentlemen 6s, ladies 4s. He paid private visits which were not confined to supporters of the government. On Wednesday 26 April he was at the Gurneys' at Earlham with a great deal of company. The other Gurneys made a great fuss about the visit and he was persuaded to come again the following Sunday to meet them.[8]

While the prince was enjoying Norwich society, the county freeholders held a meeting in the city to petition for the removal of His Majesty's Ministers. Robert Fellowes making the proposal spoke of the unexampled misfortunes suffered under a virtuous monarch—a loyal people defended by a brave and disciplined army and a navy whose brilliant exploits rivalled those of the most glorious periods of our history. Their misfortunes could only be ascribed to the misconduct and incapacity of the ministers who neither inspired His Majesty's enemies with dread nor his people with confidence. Thomas William Coke spoke attributing much evil to the overgrown influence of the crown.

Three days later the supporters of the government held a counter-demonstration when Sir Thomas Beevor moved the address. Despite a good deal of noise Mark Wilks succeeded in moving an amendment which won the support of about one third of those present. Other opponents tried to speak but were told that the meeting was dissolved and any speaker would risk the rigours of the Sedition Act.[9]

A month later the prince, accompanied by Alderman Robert Harvey junior and John Patteson, made a tour of the county. On 2 May they were at Holkham where they partook of a "sumptuous collation".[10] No doubt, after his recent speech T. W. Coke wished to show his hospitality equal to the expectations of royalty. Back in Norwich the prince was initiated into the membership of a convivial society—the ancient and honourable order of Gregorians. Speaking to them after dinner he regretted that he would soon have to leave Norwich, a city to be revered for its loyalty to the King, its attachment to the Constitution and its distinguished hospitality. The quarterly assembly of the Corporation in May voted the freedom of the city to the prince and to Admiral Nelson and the former left to take command at Ipswich promising a return visit.

Norwich reformers were still active and at the beginning of May determined on action similar to that taken by the Norfolk freeholders. "Several respectable gentlemen" requested the Mayor to convene a Common Hall to consider an address for the removal of the present administration. The respectable gentlemen were Bartlett Gurney, Dr Rigby, William Barnard, W. W. Wilkin a grocer and a dissenter, William Unthank an attorney, James Crowe the mayor-elect and his son-in-law Sigismund Trafford who had already taken part in the free-holders' meeting.[11] When the Common Hall was duly assembled on 16 May 1797 Trafford moved the petition saying that during the present contest larger demands had been made on the property of the people than ever before while greater calamities had fallen on the nation than in any former war. There had been injurious encroachments on British liberty while taxes grievously oppressed the industrious poor and even deprived the middle classes of many domestic comforts. John Pitchford said there were two parties in Norwich opposed to the ministry—those who wished merely for peace and those who thought radical reform necessary. Norwich was known among Mr Pitt's friends as the "Jacobin city". The present calamities, he argued, originated in the unequal representation of the people. Hudson Gurney attacked the conduct of the war —none of its objectives had been achieved. Mark Wilks said that the King, formerly universally beloved, had lost the esteem of the people, a change produced by the men who had supported the American war and continued the present con-flict. His Majesty's happiness—his very existence—depended on a change of men and measures. The petition for removal of the ministers was carried unanimously save for the opposition of one spirited individual.[12] A counter address was got up by the other party speaking of the blessed work His Majesty's Ministers were zealous to accomplish.

The war was brought home to the citizens at this time by the arrival of a party of French prisoners landed at Yarmouth and on their way to Norman's Cross. They were lodged in the Castle for two nights where their officers were provided with beds "through the humanity of the debtors". They were visited by numbers of curious citizens and eventually marched out of the city singing the "Marseillois". Another party passing through in September "met with most humane attention from Mr Amand, keeper of the Castle".

Opposition now appeared at a new level. On 24 May handbills described as "most scandalous, wicked and seditious", were thrown into the barracks yard of the Inniskillings and under the barracks gate of the Oxfordshire Militia. At this time the fleet at the Nore was in a state of mutiny and the authorities greatly feared disaffection in the army. The major of the Oxfordshire Militia assembled his men and after congratulating them on having their attachment to their King and officers and their country put on trial, offered a free discharge to any who wished it. The men then agreed to subscribe three days pay to a reward for anyone securing the conviction of the perpetrator of the handbills.

Just about this time Thelwall arrived back in Norwich and announced his intention of resuming his classico-political lectures. This led to disturbances which were described by Joseph Kinghorn in a letter dated Thursday 1 June.

> Some soldiers have completely gutted 2 public houses where the Democrats held their Clubs & met to drink porter & read the papers. The Landlord of one is very much hurt his family put into dreadfull terrors, many people got black eyes & broken heads, & the whole city was thrown into a panic. . . . The day being the 29 of May —Thelwall intending to deliver a political lecture that evening at a room near these houses, . . . & the soldiers intending to shew their regard to King & Constitution & an opposition to some hand bills which have been circu-

lated thro the kingdom in every Regiment—perhaps too
being irritated at the foolish things they might have heard
from the Democrats who are not famous for the discretion
of their conversation—all might operate & possibly some
other causes hid from public eye might further operate to
induce them to riot. They were of the Inniskilling reg^t.
of Horse an Irish and a desperate regiment, so much so
that their officers have oft complained of the difficulty of
keeping them under subjection. . . . The riotous state of
the Navy makes it more difficult to preserve authority in
the army than it has been. The place of the riot was . . .
near Gurney's bank. . . . The civil Magistrates were quite
frightened, as indeed they commonly are in any real danger.
They can swagger in their gowns to Church or to the
Halls either to dine or talk about trivial things & they can
hang a poor thief whom a Judge has condemned & whom
nobody tries to rescue . . . but when activity is required &
courage is wanted they are as bad as a parcell of old women.

Thelwall escaped and fled to London. The ring-leaders among
the soldiers were never identified but Luke Rice, a tailor, was
capitally indicted for aiding and encouraging them to demolish
the Shakespeare Tavern. Eventually he was acquitted through
some fault in the indictment. A few weeks later when the
Mayor, William Herring, went out of office, the Common
Councilmen shewed their resentment at his handling of the
business of the riot by staying away from the Assembly of the
Corporation so that there could be no vote of thanks for his
services.

When William Herring had been elected Mayor the year
before he was the only alderman who had not previously
served and so was due for appointment. But the radical freemen
tried hard to get two whigs—Aldermen Crowe and Norgate—
nominated and so compel the Court to appoint a Blue and
White supporter. Their ploy failed and Herring was duly
elected. This year the freemen's nominees were two senior
aldermen—James Crowe, a whig, and Robert Harvey, a tory.
For reasons of their own neither of them wished for the
mayoralty and in the end Crowe was elected by a solid tory

vote, his whig friends voting against his appointment.[13] Apart from being opposed to the government, Crowe was a notable botanist and was married to one of the Beevor family. At the time of taking office he was ill and had to be sworn at his house at Lakenham. In these circumstances the Guild Day celebrations including the Mayor's feast were abandoned. Crowe's friend Elias Norgate wrote an obituary of "Dame Letitia Guild" which was published in the local papers. She had, he said, preserved her character spotless whilst a witness to some excesses in her guests. Amid the wreck of empires and the crash of thrones her loss must excite alarming apprehensions.[14]

A week after assuming office Crowe received a letter from the Duke of Portland warning him that the London Corresponding Society had announced a meeting on 31 July on the pretext of an address to the nation on the right of the people to universal suffrage and equal representation. They had invited affiliated societies to meet the same day. The Duke called on all magistrates to put into force the Act for preventing seditious meetings. Crowe was able to reply that he had read the letter to the magistrates but that they knew of no illegal meetings intended to be held.[15] It seems likely enough that he would have been able to arrange matters with the leaders of the Patriotic Society. In the parallel case at Nottingham, the whig Corporation there allowed such a meeting to be held in the market place where it passed without any disturbance.

Deprived of this excitement, the city was enlivened the next day by a parade of the Loyal Military Association. They assembled at 8 a.m. at St Andrew's Hall, marched to Surrey St where Col. Bulwer presented their colours in front of the house of their commander John Patteson. They then marched to Mousehold heath to go through various evolutions and on their return were regaled with dinner at Neech's Gardens at their officer's expense.

In July 1797 the Patriotic Society took advantage of a visit to London by their late president R. N. Waite, an ironmonger and brazier, to transmit an expression of civic friendship to their correspondents. They expressed themselves convinced that annual parliaments and a free representation were the only basis for the happiness of man in his political state.[16] In

August with the Rev. Stephen Weavers Browne, as their
president—he had just succeeded William Bossley, a leather
dresser—they issued an address to their fellow citizens. They
boldly confessed themselves advocates of innovation. Had it
not been for this man must still have been "naked and ignorant,
the tenant of the woods". They did not conclude that all
wisdom died with their forefathers.

> As to France, the spectacle of a brave and high-spirited
> people—who have determined to be free—being able to
> brave the storm; to rise superior to all opposition and
> maintain their independency is highly interesting to those
> who can see in that event the dark clouds of moral evil
> disappearing and the bright orb of liberty advancing in
> meridian splendour.

The present war they considered unnecessary in its origins and
most fatal to the interests of the country. They considered the
following to be obstacles to more liberal and beneficial political
plans—the imposition of tythes; the vexatious practices of the
Law Courts; the modes of punishing criminals; and the right
of primogeniture. They asserted that no imperious threat or
artful insinuations should deter them from the discharge of
their duties.[17]
About the same time as the publication of this manifesto
Richard Dinmore junior, probably the son of the former
president of the Patriotic Society, published "An Exposition
of the Principles of the English Jacobins". Their enemies, he
said, called them Jacobins to confuse the public mind. They did
not approve the proceedings of that fell monster Robespierre.
Theirs were not French principles—though the French had
acted upon them. They derived from Locke, Sydney, Marvel,
Milton, &c. Their aim was to assist the poor and needy, to
lessen the horrors of the dungeon, to uprear the olive branch
of peace and to teach men to do unto others as they would they
should do to them. They objected to enormous salaries for the
idle while the laborious had scarce enough. Valiant soldiers
and hardy seamen should have more—commanders less. They
opposed laws cramping industry and detested the Game Laws.
On religion they were agreed to differ. Each sect should support

its own clergy but the labour of the industrious should not be used to pamper fat bishops, lazy deans, idle prebendaries or drowsy rectors. The Jacobins venerated the law but cases might occur when it was the duty of every man to risk his life to preserve his country's rights—as for example Washington in America. They had been wrongfully accused of seeking the death of the King. They considered their present gracious Sovereign the best of Princes, but a profligate ministry had expended £300m in two wars, each against the rights and happiness of a people and in each of which the King had lost 100,000 subjects. The crimes for which a sanguinary British annually consigned numbers of her sons to the gallows, the Jacobins attributed to poverty. They would amend the situation of the poor and open national schools where they might learn useful knowledge, sound morality and rational principles of government. They would abolish hanging and public whipping.[18]

Dinmore himself seems not to have been sanguine of the success of the Jacobins—he said that he intended to emigrate to America.* His pamphlet has a slight note of disillusion— earlier Jacobins had tended to excuse rather than deplore the excesses of the French.

The Assize week that August had an added attraction in that Prince William Fredrick had accepted an invitation to stay with John Patteson in Surrey St to take part in the festivities. His programme included a concert of Handel's music at the Cathedral in aid of the Norfolk and Norwich Hospital and a dinner with the Grand Jury. He reviewed the Loyal Military Association and was installed Grand by the Gregorians. The Assize resulted in four capital convictions. Davey, the land-lord of the Shakespeare Inn, sued the Chief Constable and city authorities for the damages he had sustained during the riots occasioned by Thelwall's lectures, and received an award. "We never remember to have witnessed such an influx of company as during the present week", noted the *Chronicle*.

In October 1797 there was more good news and the Mayor's

---

* Richard Dinmore in fact went to America. In 1802 he published in Washington City a Compilation of Select and Fugitive Poetry with notes historical and biographical and a commendatory note from Thomas Jefferson.

Court paid St Peter's ringers £2 2s 0d for ringing on Admiral
Duncan's victory over the Dutch Fleet.[19] Many wounded seamen from this battle were brought here and admitted to the
Norfolk and Norwich Hospital and the Mayor called a meeting
to raise a subscription for their relief. By mid-November the
surgeons were prepared to allow sixty of the "brave tars" to be
regaled in Keymer's Pantheon with true English fare—roast
beef, plum-pudding and tobacco with sufficient porter for a
good digestion. Spectators were admitted to the feast on
payment of six pence towards the fund for widows and orphans
of sailors.[20]

About this time Prince William Fredrick came back to
Norwich to take command of the district, a house in Bracondale
being fitted up for him. He dined with P. M. Martineau the
surgeon. He subscribed £5 to the prisoners in the city gaol and
the same to the debtors in the Castle for beef, bread and beer.
On 23 December, thanks-giving day for Admiral Duncan's
victory, he heard the Dean preach in the Cathedral and the
same evening went to a party at the Herrings'—William
Herring who had been Mayor in the previous year and lived in
St Giles in the big house, now the Y.M.C.A. The Gurney girls
were at this party and Richenda noted that it was entertaining
seeing everybody flirt and look so silly. Five days later the
prince was at Earlham and enjoyed himself enough to keep his
carriage waiting at the door for two hours. He attended other
social functions and early in January paid a final visit to
Earlham, when:

> He insisted that Rachel should preach him a sermon. He
> and a great many more of us ran up to Betsy's room and
> Rachel gave a most capital sermon. I never saw anything
> so droll as it was to see the Prince and all of us locked up
> in Betsy's room and Rachel preaching to him, which she
> did in her most capital manner, giving him a good lesson
> in the Quakers' strain and imitating William Crotch to
> perfection.[21]

On 13 January 1798, as the *Norfolk Chronicle* noted, the
Prince having executed his military duties and honoured with
his company most of the principal families in the city left to

assume command at Canterbury. Captain Patteson gave him a farewell dinner and he did not leave Norwich till midnight.

About this time Norwich entertained a very different visitor in William Winterbotham, a Baptist minister of Plymouth, who had recently been released from prison after serving a sentence for exciting His Majesty's subjects to sedition in two sermons. The judge, who had summed up rather in Winterbotham's favour, had warned the jury that should they convict him he would be utterly ruined. In this the learned judge was mistaken. The conviction earned him a measure of fame and a place in the *Dictionary of National Biography* which he would scarcely have achieved had he been acquitted. Joseph Kinghorn, writing on 9 January gave this account of the visit:

> He has preached for Mr Newton [Old Meeting, Independant] Mr Wilks & myself and all classes of men have been eager to hear him. I have been at different times in his company. . . . He is a popular preacher & by that means likely to be a very usefull one. Not a man of extensive and keen research. . . . Many people more happy because less nice think what they have heard quite good & great. I freely allow the first but not the last. Part of the popularity he has attained doubtless arises from his having been persecuted. . . . The postures of attention expressed by uplifted eyes stretched out necks & chins, to hear what the man who had been 4 years in Newgate should say, was sometimes fit to get the better of my gravity.

Meanwhile there was danger of a French invasion. Leave had been stopped and the supplementary militia partly embodied. Pitt, to meet the crisis, had introduced the biggest budget in the country's history with enormous increases in taxation. Charles James Fox, fresh from three weeks at Holkham where the party had accounted for 2700 partridges, declared that the taxes would annihilate trade and property. Yet the Finance Bill was passed on 5 January 1798 and the Speaker suggested that the pill of compulsory taxation might be sweetened by additional voluntary contributions. Following this suggestion a number of tory citizens requisitioned the Mayor for a Common Hall. This was convened at the Guildhall on 21 February.

Crowe, as Mayor, opened the proceedings but as his sentiments did not coincide with those of the assembly he left the chair to his predecessor William Herring. The meeting passed a vote of thanks to him for convening them—he replied that the thanks of so respectable a meeting must ever be acceptable, and with that he withdrew. The meeting then resolved to open a subscription to support public credit and to meet the threatened danger. Roger Kerrison and Son thereupon subscribed £500, William Herring, Robert Harvey junior and John Patteson £200 each. In all £2200 was promised that day. The Court of Aldermen, despite the opposition of the Mayor and Alderman Norgate, were prepared to subscribe but the Common Council rejected the proposition. The servants at John Patteson's house sent £5 15s 6d: the employees at his Pockthorpe Brewery £42 6s 6d. Most dissenters were opposed to giving aid to the government but Samuel Fisher's Baptist congregation in Pottergate St sent £20 in acknowledgement of privileges enjoyed under the mild government of his present Majesty and their utter detestation of French liberty and all its concomitants.[22] Although with few exceptions the voluntary contribution was boycotted by the whigs, over £8000 was raised before the appeal closed.

The more active citizens were busy preparing themselves to resist invasion and the government was prepared to encourage them. Volunteers doing six hours a week training were to be entitled to 1s a week if they saw fit to claim it. The Light Horse Volunteers unanimously agreed that their services should be given freely and further that they would march anywhere His Majesty directed.[23]

By April the Lord Lieutenant had laid plans for moving stocks and population in case of invasion and James Crowe, no doubt criticised for opposing financial help to the government, was saying he was sure the city would be unanimous in its effort against the common enemy. Norwich, he said, had been much calumniated. Notwithstanding the number of their poor, they had shewn themselves as loyal and peaceable as anywhere in the kingdom. The feelings of the time are described in a letter written by Kinghorn on 1 May 1798.

We have been quite in a ferment about the late new Act

concerning Arming, and a great nº. in most of our parishes
have entered into Associations to arm & be trained, but a
great deal of this is that they may avoid as much as possible
the power of Government by being Volunteers and pre-
scribing as far as they can their own terms. They had
rather associate agreeing to defend themselves and each
other within the limits of Norwich & its boundaries (wᶜ.
make in all a circle of about 5 miles diameter) than give in
their names to Government to be ruled by it altogether.

It is surprising, he says, how the talk of invasion has worked
its way into everything so that "if the French do not come" is
the condition on which many things are suspended.

The day before Kinghorn wrote this 62 parishioners of
St John Maddermarket signed an offer of their services. They
wished to manifest their attachment to the King and to protect
their religion, laws and liberties from the attempts of a daring
and insidious foe by forming a corps of volunteer infantry to
defend the city, police it and preserve internal tranquility.
They made it a condition that they should not be called out of
the city nor be liable to be drafted into any other corps. Each
man was to find his own uniform and would receive no pay.
They undertook to train twice a week for two hours at a time.
Their proposals were transmitted to the Lord Lieutenant by their
Captain-elect, James Boyce, an attorney. About the same time
Lord Townshend received similar proposals from a number of
other parishes. He set on foot enquiries into the bona fides of
those concerned, and consulted Henry Hobart on the matter.
As a result he would not recommend the application from
St John Maddermarket "not having assurance that they are
zealously attached to the Government".[24] In fact Boyce was a
consistent tory though the majority of those whose names
appear both on the lists of volunteers and in the Poll Books
were blue-and-white voters. Lord Townshend sent an unqualified recommendation to Secretary Dundas of the proposed
corps for the parishes of St Peter's Mancroft, St Stephen's,
St Peter's PerMountergate, St Saviour's with St Clement's,
St George's Tombland and St Lawrence's. He considered the
suggested personnel of St Andrew's as "eligible and proper"

except for their proposed Ensign, Robert Harmer, who was "very improper". Harmer was a consistent anti-government voter. No doubt it was for the same reason that the Lord Lieutenant "from the information received from a great many impartial persons of the first respectability" felt himself not justified in recommending the volunteers from St George's Colegate and St Michael's Coslany, both hot-beds of radicalism. The projectors of the St Andrew's corps were much upset by the hold-up of their recognition—they were probably unaware of the objection raised to Robert Harmer. Support fell away and in July the officers, Harmer included, issued a printed letter to the parishioners saying that permission for the corps would have been received sooner but for the interference of someone interested in their humiliation. Their characters and proceedings had been grossly misrepresented to the government and now those parishioners who were failing to come forward were affording a triumph to those who had taken pains to degrade them.[25] The invasion scare had by now evaporated and St Andrew's was only able to muster 30 of its original 70 volunteers.

The military enthusiasm had its effect on trade. John Oxley in the market place offered to supply gentlemen forming military associations with gold and silver laces, epaulets, swordknots and belts, silk and worsted sashes, and regimental colours. Dunham and Yallop had an assortment of muskets and swords. G. King, in London Lane, offered breastplates and military saddles and J. B. Bolingbroke blue and scarlet broadcloths.

This summer the corporation chose John Browne to be Mayor, a tory in place of the whig James Crowe. John Browne was treasurer of the Norwich Voluntary Contribution, captain of the St Peter's Mancroft volunteers and in business an ironmonger. Mayoral hospitality which had been in abeyance the previous year was revived with a sumptuous entertainment in St Andrew's Hall when 556 sat down to dinner. Browne does not seem to have regarded his elevation as a party victory. Among the toasts drunk at his feast was: "May our spirit and unanimity command a safe and honourable peace."

If a tory could talk of peace, many whigs were becoming

disillusioned with France as a model of political wisdom. Kinghorn, who though no politician had been a supporter of the revolution, wrote:

> The French are now awfull scourges on the continent. . . . Exaggeration is very common among men and it is probable they are not so black as they are by some described But besides their cruelties, w^c. are unequalled by anything lately in Europe—their being most of them Infidels & many of them Atheists professedly in all the higher or (according to present times) the more active ranks of Society, and their having strumpets drawn in processions as Goddesses &c &c—is I believe quite true. . . . All those notions of liberty w^c. the French Revolution very generally raised a few years ago are at an end, they are the tyrants not the deliverers of men. Yet I think we ought to believe with caution the reports about their designs, for it is certainly the interest of our Governors that the people should be very much frighted just now, as money will flow much more readily from the influence of that passion than of any other.

Even that great supporter of the Revolution, William Taylor, could write that autumn in a letter to the poet Southey:

> I grow very anti-gallican. I dislike the cause of national ambition and aggrandisment as much as I liked the cause of national representation and liberty.[26]

Unknown to people at home, on 1 August Nelson had destroyed the French fleet in Aboukir Bay. The news did not reach Norwich until 2 October when St Peter's bells were rung deliriously all day. This victory reinforced a few weeks later by Sir John Warren's capture of the greater part of a French Squadron on its way to Ireland provided an excuse for celebrations over two whole months, celebrations which were so boisterous that the Court of the Mayoralty had to issue a warning that persons throwing fireballs or squibs in the streets on rejoicing nights would be prosecuted and that householders should not allow muskets or pistols to be fired from their houses.[27] Mr and Mrs John Berry gave an elegant ball at the

Assembly House in honour of Nelson and their brother
Edward Berry his captain. This ball was supported by the
Mayor and 200 guests who retired reluctantly between two and
three in the morning.[28] The Mayor set on foot a subscription
for the relief of the widows and orphans of the battle of the
Nile, which unlike the voluntary contribution, drew support
from whigs as well as tories. When the authentic account of the
battle reached the city on 22 October the bells were rung again
and a French tricolour was flown from St Peter's tower with a
Union Jack over it. The Assembly of the Corporation actually
achieved unanimity on a humble address to the King sending
warmest congratulations on Nelson's most glorious and
important victory.

> To this achievement with other signal successes of your
> majesty's navy and aided by the loyal and gallant spirit
> displayed by your people, we ascribe the enjoyment of our
> internal security and the preservation of our inestimable
> constitution. . . .

They further resolved to ask Lord Nelson to sit for his
portrait.[29] This was in due course painted by Sir William
Beechey, R.A., exhibited in the 1801 Academy and hung in
St Andrew's Hall.

29 November being appointed the official thanksgiving day,
the Mayor, Aldermen and Sheriffs in their carriages followed
the various corps of volunteers to the Cathedral. On their
return to the market place, the volunteers formed up round a
50 stone ox which was roasting. The ox was then cut up and
distributed to the populace together with six barrels of beer.
That night the city was extensively illuminated, even Bracondale Hill being "one blaze of light". Upwards of fifty houses
were adorned with transparencies—scenes of diaphanous
material lit from behind lamps or candles—many of them
designed by the artist John Ninham. Even Gurney's Bank,
the leading whig institution, was splendidly lighted and a
number of whigs were among those displaying transparencies,
among them Edmund Cotman in Cockey Lane and the Rev.
Thomas Drummond in St George's Tombland. Drummond
displayed the signs of the zodiac with the planets in their

positions as at the time of the engagement in appropriate
colours of transparent silk. A favourite theme for the transparencies was Britannia ruling the waves. Edward Colman,
the surgeon, displayed one with a pile of cannon-balls and the
inscription, "British pills effectively employed in the case of
the French disease". A conversation piece shewn by Mr Sheriff
Tawell represented the "Jacobin Club or Hell upon Earth"
with the Devil presiding over Brissot and Robespierre with
Tom Paine and Dr Priestley in attendance.[30]

The euphoria of these celebrations was forgotten with the
onset of a long hard winter. Early in December the United
Friars Society began their annual distribution of soup and
bread to the poor. The cold increased and on 29 December a
temperature of 4°F below zero was recorded in the city.
Kinghorn wrote: "Here everything liquid froze everywhere
except at the fireside—Water—Beer even the Chamber-pots
under the beds all froze in a manner seldom known." The
Norfolk Chronicle recommended flannel waistcoats as the most
useful charity for the poor. Besides the extreme cold snow held
up transport and the coaches which should have reached
Norwich on Saturday 2 February 1799 did not arrive till the
following Tuesday night.

The party truce induced by the victories of 1798 was ended
and the whig gentry to counteract, they said, a torrent of abuse
against Charles James Fox, celebrated his birthday by a dinner
at the Angel with Sigismund Trafford in the chair. Among the
toasts drunk were: The Sovereignty of the People; The
triumphant reestablishment of the Habeas Corpus Act; May
no aristocratic folly impede a safe and honourable peace; The
tars of old England; and Independance and Prosperity to the
City of Norwich.[31]

For many the weather was too hard for politics. The cold
persisted into April and conditions were exacerbated in
Norwich by a shortage of coals—various reasons were alleged
for this misfortune, among them the quantities being shipped
by the East India Company to the Cape.[32]

In May 1799 Henry Hobart, the city's senior M.P., died at
Bath. In the resultant bye-election both sides saw fit to choose
country gentlemen as their candidates. The tories' choice was

John Frere F.R.S. of Royden. His son John Hookham Frere was already in Parliament, was concerned with Canning in the publication of *The Anti-Jacobin* and had been appointed Under-secretary of State in the Foreign Office that April. Frere at once wrote to Robert Fellowes of Shottesham saying that he wished to save the city from the disgrace of a jacobinical representation and asking his support as an old friend. Fellowes, who belonged to the other party, replied that he knew no gentleman better qualified than Frere for a seat in Parliament nor any truer friend of the religion and constitution they equally venerated. He had himself had conversations with respectable gentlemen at Norwich and could make no promises. A few days later he himself emerged as the whig candidate. Frere's partisans printed Fellowes' letter and taxed him with having as his supporters men who had corresponded with the French National Convention—naming particularly William Barnard and John Cozens.

Fellowes enjoyed a good deal of local support as Treasurer of the Norfolk and Norwich Hospital which his father had founded but the whigs' opposition to the war was not so popular as it had been before the victories of 1798. The tories were able to claim that Frere was supporting the men who were forcing the French to make peace whereas Fellowes' timid advice, if followed, would have sacrificed the country's best interests and made its commerce and manufactures over to the enemy. Polling was on 27 May when Frere won by 1345 botes to 1186. Fellowes actually polled three more resident Norwich votes than his rival. Both candidates brought about 100 voters from London, an expense which had not been incurred on that scale since 1787, but Frere was far more successful than Fellowes in attracting voters in from the country.

Frere in an address to the citizens said he valued the victory the more because it had been obtained over a party who, whatever their good intentions, had been misled by vain theories to foster principles and recommend measures which in the present state of Europe were invariably destructive in tendency. He thought too that the personal merits and public services of his opponent had attracted support.

Recruiting for the volunteers went on that summer, the

various patriotic corps, the *Chronicle* said, increasing in numbers and respectability. On the King's birthday they paraded in force to the cathedral, after which the Light Horse dined at the King's Head, Major Patteson's corps at Neech's Gardens and the Mancroft Volunteers at Back's Bowling Green. On Guild Day Major Patteson's men were formed up on the market place and fired three vollies in honour of the new Mayor John Herring. Parson Woodforde did not think much of him and noted of the occasion, "Not much genteel company expected to be there". Actually the Mayor's feast was notable for the presence of Sir Edward Berry, who after being toasted himself, got up and proposed the health of the Mayor and Mayoress and Prosperity to the city of Norwich. Herring proved an active and effective Mayor. He sought to keep down food prices by discouraging forestalling in the city's markets. He succeeded in banishing from the streets "those wretched females with whom the city too much abounds". But his chief claim to fame was his dealing with the emergency which arose when large numbers of troops repatriated from Holland arrived at Yarmouth and were routed through Norwich. The government which had hurried the ill-equiped expedition to the Helder at the end of August, by the middle of October became convinced of the necessity of abandoning the venture. An armistice had been arranged and evacuation proceeded.

On Tuesday morning 29 October Herring was warned of their coming. At 8 p.m. the same evening 800 of the Guards reached the city. They were met at Bishop's bridge, conducted to the market place with flambeaux and billeted at inns and public houses. The Mayor was present to keep an eye on the operation and, said the *Mercury* reporter, the populace seemed anxious to alleviate the fatigue of the soldiers, women and boys compassionately conducting them to their quarters and carrying their gear. The reporter talked to the Guards who, he said, were the finest body of men in the English service and in excellent health and spirit. They were unanimous in testifying to the bravery of the French troops. Their Russian allies they thought more eager for plunder than victory. The Dutch were universally abhorred—they were unwilling even to sell provisions.[33]

Next day the Guards moved on and more troops arrived. In the course of ten days no less than 7682 cavalry, infantry and camp-followers were billeted and sent on their way. The Mayor was thanked by the government. It was rumoured that he was offered a baronetcy but declined it.

In the days of sail when Yarmouth was a major port, Norwich was on an important line of communication with the continent. That November, close on the heels of the troops from Holland, came Baron Jacobi, minister of the court of Berlin. He paid his respects to the Mayor, visited Mr Knight's shawl manufactory and rested the night at the Angel before posting to London, leaving behind him a rumour of a negotiation for a general peace.[34]

REFERENCES

1. C. L. Brightwell, *Life of Amelia Opie*, p. 58.
2. *Norfolk Chronicle*, 25 Feb. 1797.
3. Court of Mayoralty Book.
4. *Norfolk Chronicle*, 11 Mar. 1797.
5. Public Record Office, H.O. 50/341.
6. Court of Mayoralty Book.
7. *Norfolk Chronicle*, 11 Mar. 1797.
8. A. J. C. Hare, *Gurneys of Earlham*, vol. I, p. 63.
9. *Norfolk Chronicle*, 29 April 1797.
10. *Norfolk Chronicle*, 6 May 1797.
11. *Norfolk Chronicle*, 13 May 1797.
12. *Norfolk Chronicle*, 20 May 1797.
13. N & N Record Office. Colman MSS, "Events in Norfolk and Suffolk".
14. *Norfolk Chronicle*, 24 June 1797.
15. Court of Mayoralty Book.
16. British Museum 27815 L.C.S. Letter Book 159.
17. Nch Local Hist. Library, Colman Collection, Address of the Patriotic Society.
18. Rich. Dinmore jnr. Exposition of the Principles of the English Jacobins.
19. Court of Mayoralty Book.
20. *Norfolk Chronicle*, 11 Nov. 1797.
21. A. J. C. Hare, op. cit., vol. I, pp. 71-3.
22. *Norfolk Chronicle*, 10 Mar. 1798.
23. *Norfolk Chronicle*, 24 Mar. 1798.
24. P.R.O., H.O. 50/341.

25. P.R.O., H.O. 50/44.
26. J. W. Robberds, *Memoir of Wm. Taylor*, vol. I, p. 229.
27. Court of Mayoralty Book.
28. *Norfolk Chronicle*, 13 Oct. 1798.
29. Assembly Book.
30. *Norfolk Chronicle*, 1 Dec. 1798.
31. *Norfolk Chronicle*, 26 Jan. 1799.
32. *Norfolk Chronicle*, 6 April 1799.
33. *Norfolk Chronicle*, 2 Nov. 1799.
34. *Norfolk Chronicle*, 23 Nov. 1799.

8 Norwich Politics 1800–1802

In January 1800 the Mayor, John Herring, started a new initiative, calling a meeting of citizens to consider acquiring powers to improve the city as to paving, cleansing, lighting and watching. Dr Rigby supported the plan but advocated the preparation of estimates before action was decided upon. Even without estimates William Barnard, another whig, opposed the plan on grounds of cost while Alderman Browne, a tory, thought it should be deferred till times were more prosperous. John Gurney and Alderman Harvey, leading members of the two parties, feared the time were not favourable. Rigby moved to appoint a committee to consider the plan and this was agreed to. 21 members were chosen fairly equally divided between the two parties and including the radical extremists Jonathon Davey and Peter Willsea.[1] The committee reported in March that the improvements were estimated to cost £55,000. A survey of traffic using the 14 principal avenues of the city for seven days shewed:

4184 horses, 4644 carts and waggons, and 829 carriages.[2]

They calculated that a toll on horses and conveyances could produce a net sum of £1715 per annum and a 6d rate £3000. On the basis of these figures the committee recommended applying for an Act of Parliament. Alderman Browne was again opposed to the plan which, he said, would increase the price of provisions. Dr Beevor was against it but Dr Rigby supported it saying that it would be favourable to the poor in saving the wear and tear of shoes. Mr Watson, the miller of Saxlingham, averred that people in the county would approve and contribute their share. The Mayor thought that the county would be pleased and he secured a majority in favour of the plan.[3] A petition was prepared and signed by a large number of citizens but for some reason it could not be presented to

Parliament that session. The project thus lost its impetus and the desired Act was not in fact obtained until 1806.

Wheat was scarce this spring and bread dear. Woodforde sent wheat to Mr Bloom at Trowse mills in February and received 57s a coomb—"The greatest Price I ever yet recd. for wheat". A few days later he heard that the price was 60s, occasioning "very great grumbling among the Poor". The United Friars Society was engaged in its annual distribution of bread and soup, giving out this winter over 28,000 tickets for a penny loaf and a quart of broth. By March the need was so great that the Mayor raised a subscription—more than £1100— and opened six soup shops where poor families could buy soup at $\frac{1}{2}$d a pint, one pint per head being allowed to families.[4] In April it was reported that 16,000 indigent poor were getting two meals a week from the Soup Institution. The permitted price of bread had been rising steadily for twelve months. An Act of Parliament laying down that no loaf was to be sold till 24 hours after baking did not check it. At the end of April 1799 a penny loaf of standard wheaten bread had to weigh 9 oz.; now a year later it reached its lowest weight, $3\frac{3}{4}$ oz. This resulted in what the papers described as "symptoms of riot" in the market. To avoid trouble the Mayor, Sheriffs and Aldermen attended by the peace officers visited the market place on Saturday 3 May and reasoned with the discontented crowds. May saw a slight improvement in the price of bread and the crisis passed.

The stationing of troops in the city was a mixed blessing. Colonel Montgomery of the 9th Foot had a dispute with a shopkeeper which ended in blows. John Harper, the hosier, had his thumb broken and the surgeon found that mortification had set in, endangering his life. The city authorities, terribly alarmed, arrested the colonel. Four hundred soldiers then assembled at the city gaol intending to release their officer. The gaoler was badly frightened but Montgomery addressed the troops from a window and ordered them to desist, which they did after giving him three cheers. In due course Harper recovered and the colonel was released. A little later on the troops proved themselves useful. There were a number of robberies on the lonely roads around Norwich and at the

Mayor's request parties of dragoons were detailed to patrol by night the roads leading into the city.[5]

The radicals, despite irate opposition—a tract of 1799 equated them with societies for the propagation of treason and sedition—celebrated Fox's birthday by the usual dinner and drank the usual toasts, this year adding "The King and Constitution" alongside "The sovereignty of the People".[6] Though disillusioned by the French they were still fascinated by what went on in Paris and now enjoyed a first hand account of the situation. William Taylor wrote to Robert Southey in February:

> Sir Robert Barclay has been here, after confinement in the Temple at Paris as a spy. When Bonaparte got the sway he was released with a thousand apologies and invited to visit the ministers and everything else in Paris. He spent about a fortnight in amusive gaiety. His account is very flattering; the lower orders are all thriving; the generals are beginning to build new palaces; the circles of the ministers' wives are the pleasantest blue-stocking clubs imaginable. Bonaparte is a small, grey-haired warworn man, very grave, very puritannical, and about to be religious. . . . Everything is cheap in France but the wages of labour.[7]

Though Norwich tories and radicals managed to live together in peace, outsiders looked askance at the jacobinical reputation of the city. Some officers newly posted from Ireland attending the theatre in March called for the National Anthem after the first play. Unluckily the after-play had started before the management understood what was being demanded and the officers, attributing this non-compliance with their wishes to the disloyalty of the Norwich audience, drew their swords and cleared the house, bruising a number of gentlemen and tearing their clothes. At Quarter Sessions the officers, four ensigns and a lieutenant of the 85th Foot, pleaded guilty to causing a riot and were fined £5 a head.[8]

The volunteer organisations continued their activities. On the fast-day in March some of them accompanied the Mayor to the cathedral to hear Prebendary Anguish preach an eloquent sermon on the text, "O thou sword of the Lord how long will it be ere thou be quiet". Others paraded to their parish churches.[9] In April the Loyal St Saviour's Volunteers received their colours and made the occasion the excuse for a convivial evening at Neech's gardens. In May some of them held a field-day on open ground outside St Stephen's gates.

Later that month in London a shot was fired at the Royal Box in Drury Lane as the King was bowing to the audience, an incident which encouraged loyalist sentiment. The United Friars Society at their meeting unanimously testified their joy, "partaking in the general happiness of the Kingdom the providential escape of His Majesty from the attempt to assasinate him". John Herring and Robert Harvey, the Mayor and Mayor-elect, travelled to London and presented the King with a congratulatory address from the corporation.

When the Common Council met in June for the installation of a new Mayor a tribute to John Herring was voiced by Samuel Stone, a whig, who remarked that, whatever difference of opinion there might be about the expedition to Holland, there could be nothing but an unqualified approbation of the Mayor's efforts on behalf of "our unfortunate bretheren" the troops returning from it.[10] The incoming Mayor, Robert Harvey, was serving a second time after a lapse of thirty years. In his honour a Triumphal Arch was ingeniously constructed near his house in St Clement's—covered with evergreens and decorated with flowers, its battlements concealing a music gallery.

The price of bread remained high all that summer. In an endeavour to keep down the price of provisions Harvey had the Guildhall bell rung at midday on market days and ordered that no foggers or retail dealers were to buy in the market till after that hour.[11] In early September there was insufficient flour and meal available for the demands of the citizens and crowds of discontented people assembled around the New Mills—the first water-mills in the city above tidal water. The Sheriffs attended by constables managed to disperse the mob without incident. The Light Horse Volunteers offered their services but were not called upon. A week later Mr Bloom the Trowse miller managed to purchase in London 400 barrels of

American flour which eased the situation a little.[12] At the end
of the month the Court of the Mayoralty was still considering
the distresses of the poor and the misconduct of the populace.
They issued a printed handbill saying that the magistrates
would exert every legal expedient to reduce the price of bread
and pointing out the ruinous consequences of riotous proceedings and unprovoked insults to individuals.[13]

Once more in November the Mayor called a meeting of
citizens to encompass means of relieving the poor and once
more it was agreed to raise a voluntary subscription so as to
avoid an increase in rates which would have hurt small rate-
payers. The Mayor and the two Members of Parliament headed
the list with gifts of £50 each. Before Christmas the magistrates
again agreed to restrict their families from the use of fine flour
in pastry and to limit bread consumption to one quartern loaf
per head per week. No one seems to have thought these
proceedings inconsistent with occasional public feasting on a
considerable scale.

The two Sheriffs sworn in October 1800 were both grocers—
James Hardy, a tory, appointed by the Mayor's court and
Jonathon Davey, a radical, a member of Mark Wilks's congregation, elected by the freemen. Davey's election could have
been upset by invoking the Test Act but no scrutiny was called
for. Both men gave dinners to celebrate the occasion. Hardy
entertained the Mayor, the Dean, many of the Aldermen and
other gentlemen, among them the whig candidate Robert
Fellowes, elegantly at his own house while 120 of Davey's
friends sat down to a sumptuous meal at the Angel. Hardy's
table displayed the savoury swan and other bonnes bouches.
Davey's friends enjoyed turtle soup and high-seasoned venison
pasties. The wines—particularly the champagne at the Angel—
were of the first quality. The desserts included pines and grapes.
However men differ in their political and religious creeds,
remarked the *Norfolk Chronicle*, all appear to agree upon the
gratification of good eating and drinking. Fellowes after
enjoying Sheriff Hardy's hospitality, went on to Davey's party
to assist in drinking the toasts which were very numerous;
among them: "May reformation prevent revolution"; "Speedy
and honourable peace with the French Republic"; "The citizens

of Norwich, may they choose magistrates for their character not for their creed"; "The poor man's rights, food and clothing for his labour".[14]

The price of bread remained high all that winter and trade was not good. In March 1801 the example of some opulent citizens was again commended in clothing themselves and their servants in Norwich stuffs.

Changes in the government were being spoken of. These took effect in March when Pitt, unable to persuade the King of the necessity of Catholic Emancipation in Ireland to which he considered himself committed, resigned the seals of office and Charles Yorke replaced William Windham as Secretary at War. The war seemed at stalemate. When Windham had presented his estimates before his resignation he admitted that operations had perforce to be limited to measures of defence. In April came some encouragement when, on the 15th, the Yarmouth mail coach arrived with colours flying, bringing news of Nelson's destruction of the Danish fleet at Copenhagen. About the same time came an account of the death of the Tsar Paul who as Woodforde put it "had long behaved bad towards England". These events nourished the hope of peace.

Although the Test Act was still in force dissenters had long served the corporation in various offices from Mayor down. The practice of the denominations differed in this matter. The Presbyterians, who provided much of the whig leadership, were not above taking the sacrament in parish churches as Elias Norgate had done before he was chosen Mayor. The discipline of the Baptists and Independants forbad their members to do so, but if they were elected and no one challenged their election they were protected by the annual Indemnity Acts and some of them took this chance. The Quakers were too scrupulous to use this loophole. John Gurney was however a leading whig and though unable to accept nomination himself was prepared to nominate others. Joseph, an even stricter Friend, could support the parliamentary candidature of his kinsman Bartlett Gurney who had left the Society. Richard Gurney the eldest of the brothers disapproved of dabbling in politics. Writing to his uncle Charles Lloyd after the Birmingham riots he declared:

> I think . . . it tends little to the Credit of the Religion of
> Church of England or the Presbyterians that their pulpits
> should be prostituted to the purposes of political Contro-
> versy from whence it is much to be apprehended that the
> late tumults have arisen.[15]

After the 1800 elections for the Common Council, Alderman
John Browne wrote an open letter to the Sheriff pointing out
that those elected ought to have been qualified by communicating in the Church of England within one year before their
election.[16] William Barnard, a dissenting councillor, replied.
He had been, he said, originally elected without his knowledge.
Did Browne now want to throw him out? For a century past,
he alleged, the citizens had accepted the services of dissenters.
They were friends of religion, therefore of the Church.[17]
When Barnard spoke of dissenters as "friends of the Church",
he meant it in a very practical sense. He himself was a regular
attendant at vestry meetings in St George's Colegate, where he
lived, meetings which voted parish rates for the repair and
upkeep of the church.

Browne's threat was given some effect in the 1801 elections.
The procedure was that the freemen of each of the four Great
Wards elected three councillors and these three nominated the
rest of the councillors required to make up the complement
for their own wards. This year the councillors for Browne's
own ward—Mancroft—put in certificates proving that they
had duly taken the sacrament, but in the Wymer ward two of
the three elected, and in the ward Over-the Water all three
were challenged. The Mayor declared them not elected but
refused to return their rivals who had polled very few votes.
The matter was argued before Lord Kenyon in the King's
Bench who upheld the Mayor's ruling, and so new elections
were ordered. The Wymer freemen then unanimously reelected
John Staff and John Procter, the two who had been objected
to before. Three councillors were unanimously elected by the
Over-the-Water freemen, among them John Britton who had
been objected to. The other two who had been challenged,
William Barnard and Joseph Scott, were included in the list of
nominated councillors. There is no evidence that any of them

had taken the sacrament in the meantime but the Test Act was not further invoked. At least two other prominent dissenters, Thomas Hawkins and William Newson both deacons of St Mary's Baptist Church, were elected and not challenged.[18] The object of this unsuccessful revival of the Test was presumably political in support of the tory party but it seems to have back-fired in the determination of the freemen to have the councillors they wanted regardless of religious adherence.

That summer (1801) there were the usual excitements—the firing of guns and ringing of bells for the King's birthday which was made an excuse for the corps of parochial volunteers to dine at various taverns—and the Guild day when an aged whig, Jeremiah Ives, was sworn Mayor a second time. In view of his age there was no Guild feast but he gave a cold collation to the Aldermen and Commons at the Guildhall. At the end of June the crowds were brought out by an event of another sort—a fire in the cathedral roof. Soldiers and workmen were mustered under the direction of Major Patteson and Captain John Harvey who carried water up to the parapets. Despite showers of molten lead and great confusion the flames were got out in two hours after 45 feet of the nave roof had been burned. The Bishop, the courtly Dr Manners Sutton, himself distributed refreshments to the soldiers and other assistants.

In August rumours of intended invasion caused the Norfolk Supplementary Militia to be embodied and the volunteers to renew their activities. The parochial Volunteer Associations met at St Andrew's Hall and marched to the Hospital Meadow where Captain William Herring read a letter from the Lord Lieutenant exhorting them to readiness for an invasion.

Once again this September the Aldermen chose a tory, Thomas Back, and the Freemen a whig, Robert Ward, for Sheriffs and once again they held their separate feasts. Ward's friends dined at the Angel on a whole buck, the gift of T. W. Coke, and drank, in addition to the usual toasts, "Confusion to the invaders of our country and resistence to all attempts on our liberty", after which they very properly toasted "Sheriff Back and his friends".

On 3 October Marsh's Expedition coach, arriving from

London at 8 a.m., brought the first intelligence of the signing of the preliminaries of peace. The news spread like wildfire. So great a crowd gathered almost immediately that the horses took fright and overturned the coach. Men of all parties congratulated one another. The volunteers assembled on the Castle hill and marched to the market place to fire a feu-de-joie. A bonfire was lit and the church bells rang. The corporation, fearing lest the celebrations might get out of hand asked the citizens to suspend illuminations till Wednesday 21 October to allow time for adequate preparation and to prevent accidents they ordered that all should refrain from firing guns or throwing squibs or fireballs and that illuminations should cease at 11 p.m. When the day of celebration came, the signal for the general illumination was given at 6 p.m. by the lighting of flambeaux on the Guildhall roof. Immediately the city was lighted up. "Welcome Peace" proclaimed the transparency on Mr Boardman's shop in the market place; "Peace" echoed the illumination on the cornice on Gurney's Bank. A huge bonfire burned on the market. The Mayor, Aldermen and Council, preceded by the regalia and followed by the volunteers paraded round it and then enjoyed wine and plum cakes at the Guildhall. The Anacreontic Society gave a musical fete at the Assembly House for which John Crome painted a large transparency. Set up at the end of the supper room it depicted Harmony crowning Peace with laurel while in the foreground the British Lion lay guarding the Olive.

The benefits of peace were at once apparent. The price of bread fell rapidly. The Guardians of the Poor who had had to pay 9s 2d a score for loaves in the July quarter, paid only 7s 6d in October and 5s 7d in January. The *Norfolk Chronicle* hopefully pointed out that income tax having now fulfilled its purpose, its continuance seemed neither politic nor necessary. In January the Mayor and Mayoress gave a ball in honour of the peace to about 300 of the principal gentry who assembled at 8 p.m. and supped at one in the morning. The occasion is thus described in the Jerningham Letters:

> The Mayor's ball was very splendid as to numbers, the dancing very much crowded in the Tea Room and a cold

supper with hot soups in the Great Room, three tables
from top to bottom and above 50 people not sitting. . . .
Mrs Ives' dame d'honneur sat by her at supper, on the
other side Miss Drake and by her that Handsome Fair
Quaker Gurney from Earlham.[19]

Despite his mistrust of the peace William Windham was
present at this ball.

In April the news of the signing of the Definitive Treaty of
Peace was the signal for another round of celebrations. This
time the march of the Loyal Military Association was preceded
by two drays carrying six barrels of Norwich porter, the gift
of Major Patteson. The porter was decanted in the market
place for drinking the King's health. On Tuesday 4 May 1802
peace was proclaimed, first from the leads of the Guildhall,
then at several other locations in the city. Joseph Gurney
celebrated the occasion in true Quaker fashion by giving a
pound of beef, a 3d loaf and a pint of beer each to 279 poor
people of his neighbourhood. The volunteers handed in their
arms. A writer to the *Norwich Mercury* suggested that the money
set aside for illuminations would be better spent in redeeming
the pawned goods of the industrious poor, but the suggestion
was not taken up. That night the illuminations were brighter
than ever and produced a flood-lighting effect. The *Mercury*
reported:

> The most striking and awful effect of the illuminations
> arose to the mind on the contemplation of the churches
> whose towers and walls wore an air of solemn stillness and
> grandeur which it is impossible adequately to describe.
> The spire of the cathedral was particularly sublime from
> the reflection of the lights on one side and the deep un-
> changing darkness on the other. . . .

William Taylor who had taken the opportunity to visit
France witnessed the illuminations in Paris. Every ledge of the
public buildings, he reported, was lighted by stout wicks set in
bowls of grease giving a huge blaze so that the buildings
seemed made of tongues of fire. Private houses had only
candles set in the windows. He found Paris more beautiful than

before and thought Bonaparte governed wisely though people were unwilling to comment on the government. He dined at Holcroft's—Thomas Holcroft was a dramatist who had been indicted for High Treason but discharged after Hardy's acquittal—where he met Tom Paine and another East Anglian, a Mr Manning who came from Diss.[20]

Other Norwich citizens took the opportunity to visit Paris. Tradition has it that Alderman Robert Harvey junior went and that he got himself presented to Bonaparte under the name of Baron Harvey—a title which stuck to him as a nickname thereafter.

While his constituents enjoyed the peace, William Windham took a very dim view of the situation. He spoke of the treaty in the Commons in the most disparaging terms. According to the report in the *Norfolk Chronicle* he said, "While in private life points of honour are attended to with the most scrupulous exactitude, a slap upon the national face or a kick upon the public posterior goes for nothing."

A thanksgiving day being appointed on 1 June. Prebendary Potter, preaching at the Cathedral averred that there had always been more to fear from the impious philosophy of the enemy than from his arms—the detestable principles which under the names of philosophy, liberty and equality tended to introduce irreligion, profligacy of manners, contempt of laws divine or human, anarchy and the severest tyranny. He gave thanks for the undeviating wisdom of His Majesty's Ministers, the heroic ardour of his fleets and armies and the happy attachment of an united people in defence of their country.

It was known that a general election was to follow. Robert Fellowes was the first to offer himself as candidate, undertaking that he would zealously concur in whatever was most likely to continue the blessings of peace. Windham and Frere then wrote to the papers promising their conscientious and disinterested adherence to their public duty. It had been rumoured that the Mayor, Jeremiah Ives, would stand with Fellowes but in the event William Smith was adopetd as the second whig candidate. William Smith (1756–1835) belonged to a family of wealthy London grocers. He had sat in parliament since 1784, first representing Sudbury and then the pocket borough of

Camelford. He was a dissenter, a reformer and an enthusiast for the French Revolution. In 1794 he had written to a friend giving his views on a possible French invasion. His friend communicated these to William Jackson, a French spy, and when Jackson was arrested Smith had been interrogated by the Privy Council. There was nothing objectionable in Smith's letter and no action was taken against him but the incident tarred him with the brush of treason and was brought up against him in this election.[21] Windham and Frere wrote to the papers that Mr Smith's political sentiments were such that they could not but consider them favourable to their cause.

The election campaign was in full swing when Guild Day came round. The new Mayor, Sir Roger Kerrison, after going to the cathedral in a new chariot with a coachman and three footmen in handsome livery, entertained 800 guests including the four candidates to a sumptuous and plentiful dinner in St Andrew's Hall. When the Mayor toasted the city Members of Parliament applause was loud and prolonged. But there was not so much enthusiasm for them in the city at large. Windham's opposition to the peace, which time would prove to be amply justified, was extremely unpopular. On the other hand Smith's vigorous opposition to the income tax which, he said, put a spy over every man's property, was likely to win him votes. The tories sought to damn the opposition by publishing as it alleged creed:

> I believe in the Liberty of France, mother of all blessing;
> . . . in the innocence of Robespierre, patron of freedom;
> and in the pure sentiments of the present First Consul of
> France . . .; I believe in the sacred passion of uncontrolled
> freedom; in the equal participation of goods and chattels;
> in the kingdom of the sovereign people, whose favour is
> everlasting. . . .

The election took place on 5 July. Windham and Frere were proposed by Aldermen Robert Harvey junior, James Hudson and John Morse; Fellowes and Smith by John Gurney and Aldermen Jeremiah Ives junior and John Buckle. The poll opened at 9 a.m. There was a great deal of confusion in the market place. A party of sailors with blue and white cockades

for a time terrorised the voters but were themselves attacked
by a party of butchers in the orange and purple interest. In
due course the combatants were disarmed by the Sheriffs.
When the poll closed at 6 p.m. the votes were:

Fellowes 1532	Windham 1356
Smith 1439	Frere 1328

Smith, at great expense, had succeeded in bringing 169
voters from London against Windham's 116, though Windham
had attracted a hundred more country voters than his opponents. The strength of the Fellowes–Smith majority was in the
resident Norwich voters. Windham and Frere wrote that it was
a triumph for Jacobin politics. Victory, they said, lay entirely
on that side, with a deduction for the effects of money and those
arts which, though practised at all times, were rarely practised
to such an extent. Windham and Frere themselves are said to
have spent no less than £8000 on this election.[22] Three weeks
later 180 friends of Fellowes and Smith met at the Assembly
House to celebrate the victory, Aldermen Crowe and Buckle
presiding at the tables. Thomas William Coke, still involved
in the scrutiny of his election campaign for the county—he was
duly returned a month later—congratulated the Norwich
electors. Added to the usual toasts was, "May the exemplary
punishment of Mr Windham and his Frere produce their
reformation". It was a great triumph for the friends of reform
in Norwich. Someone called for, "The 5th. of July and may it
be annualy celebrated".

It is a sobering thought that the victory of the Norwich
radicals after so many years' advocacy of a creed that was widely
disliked and thought dangerous, came with a phoney peace and
largely through the efforts of a man who, while espousing the
radical cause, achieved success largely by the old corrupt
methods of electioneering. Yet there was an enduring wisdom
in the principles the radicals stood for and they built a liberal
tradition which was to play an important part in the life of the
city during the coming century.

The peace which had been hailed with so much joy soon
foundered, as William Windham had foreseen, under the
threats and demands of Bonaparte. By May 1803 the country

was once more at war with France but this time all the former
"Jacobins" were on the side of the government. To a man they
subscribed to a voluntary contribution for the defence of the
realm and when the Norwich Volunteer Regiment of Infantry
was formed that summer Sigismund Trafford and William
Firth were among its captains and John Pitchford one of its
ensigns.

REFERENCES

1. *Norfolk Chronicle*, 1 Feb. 1800.
2. *Norfolk Chronicle*, 1 Mar. 1800.
3. *Norfolk Chronicle*, 8 Mar. 1800.
4. *Norfolk Chronicle*, 15 Mar. 1800.
5. *Norfolk Chronicle*, 18 Jan. and 15 Feb. 1800.
6. *Norfolk Chronicle*, 1 Feb. 1800.
7. J. W. Robberds, op. cit., p. 331.
8. Quarter Sessions Book.
9. *Norfolk Chronicle*, 15 Mar. 1800.
10. *Norfolk Chronicle*, 21 June 1800.
11. *Norfolk Chronicle*, 2 Aug. 1800.
12. *Norfolk Chronicle*, 13 Sept. 1800.
13. *Norfolk Chronicle*, 27 Sept. 1800.
14. *Norfolk Chronicle*, 4 Oct. 1800.
15. Friend's House Library, Gurney MSS.
16. *Norwich Mercury*, 10 May 1800.
17. *Norwich Mercury*, 17 May 1800.
18. Assembly Minute Book 1790–1805.
19. Cozens, Hardy and Kent, *Mayors of Norwich*, p. 139.
20. J. W. Robberds, op. cit., pp. 403–17.
21. R. W. Davis, *Dissent in Politics 1780–1830*, pp. 71–4.
22. B. D. Hayes, *Politics in Norfolk 1750–1832*, p. 433.

9 *Shops and Shopkeeping*

Norwich with its 40,000 inhabitants seems to have been well furnished with shops. The directories published in 1783 and 1802 list some 40 grocers' shops, upwards of 30 butchers and 60 bakers, more than 30 drapers and mercers, besides two dozen hatters, hosiers, haberdashers and milliners, a dozen booksellers and half a dozen "chymists" or druggists. Both directories claim to be lists of the principal inhabitants so we may suppose there were a number of shops besides kept by people who could not be so designated.

To survey the shopping scene we may imagine a stroll through the centre of the city from Tombland to the Haymarket, remembering that in those days shopping was a very personal activity as between the shopkeeper and his customers who were usually aware of his political and religious affiliations and other peculiarities. At the corner of Queen's St with Tombland was Thomas Hawkins's grocery. Like most other tradesmen Hawkins lived over his shop with Martha his wife and their growing family who might be allowed to play in the yard of the French Church behind the shop, safe from the traffic of the street. Though situated so near the Cathedral gate Thomas Hawkins was a Baptist and his religious persuasion certainly affected his trade. He received visits from Richard Fishwick, a Baptist from Newcastle, whose firm Walker Fishwick and Co. supplied white-lead paint and lead shot. The latter was handled by the grocers and was an important commodity in the sporting county of Norfolk. Fishwick's price in 1792 was 20s 6d per cwt ex ship at Yarmouth.

On Fishwick's recommendation Hawkins persuaded his church to invite Joseph Kinghorn to become their minister. Kinghorn had started his career as a clerk in Fishwick's lead-works and subsequently studied at the Baptist Academy at Bristol. His learning and saintliness were to become a legend in Norwich; in the meantime his connections in the north proved useful to Hawkins's trade. On visits to his parents in Yorkshire he undertook the purchase of dried fruit from Hull merchants, not always a simple business. In 1796 he was buying fruit from Mr Levet who, Hawkins complained, allowed him insufficient tare and charged him 3s 6d a ton gross weight for shipping—"more than ever known". All the same he wanted Kinghorn to buy another butt of Black Smyrnas from Levet at 36s or better. Levet had offered him foreign starch but he could not get his customers to use it. Hawkins also bought butter from Kinghorn's connections at Newcastle and had it shipped by coasters to Yarmouth.

Further up Queen's St was the shop of James Nosworthy. He started as a hairdresser with perfumery and Dutch toys as side lines. In 1790 he was making têtes and chignons agreeable to the newest fashions from 5s to £5 5s od. A year later he was describing himself as a Perfumer, Dealer in Toys, Hardware, Tonbridge ware, Gold trinkets &c. He offered rocking horses from £1 1s od to £3 3s od, baby houses up to £5 5s od and wax dolls up to £1 1s od. Hairdressing was still carried on—in 1793 he announced that ladies' hairdressers were kept who might be depended on. His was a favourite shop with Parson Woodforde who frequently recorded purchases there—washballs, a puzzling fan for Nancy, a very large umbrella costing 16s, Venice soap and a shaving brush among them. When Woodforde came into Norwich in April 1793 and found all the rooms taken at the King's Head, Nosworthy obliged him with two beds.

> Nancy's bed was very good & in a good Room but mine was so bad, without curtains in a large long dark Room that I only laid down on the bed & clothes on.

They had however an excellent breakfast and the Nosworthys were very civil, so much so that besides paying the substantial bill of £1 2s 10d and giving 3s to the maids Woodforde sent them a fat green goose "as a token of their civilities".[1]

Not all the Queen's St tradesmen kept on good terms with the worthy parson. William Forster, a tailor and robe maker at the corner of St Michael's at Plea churchyard, grew weary of keeping his book uncrossed and had the effrontery to write to Woodforde asking for payment £3 18s 11d. Ben was promptly despatched to settle the account while his master dined on a boiled fowl and pork and beef steaks. When Ben came back with a receipted bill the parson recorded that he had done with Forster for ever for his late shabby ungentlemanlike behaviour which he could only account for by supposing him to be a Presbyterian.[2]

From Queen's St we cross over Bank Place, as it was then called, to London Lane with the Gurney's imposing bank house on our left. Richard, John and Joseph Gurney had already moved out of the city but Bartlett Gurney still lived next to the bank. There were four other local banks to which Harvey and Hudson's and Sir Roger Kerrison's were the best established and held between them most of the accounts of Norwich Corporation. The Gurney partners were radicals and dissenters which recommended them to important elements in Norwich industry, though by no means all their customers were of the same persuasion. The partners were men of intelligence, vigour and integrity and their bank was a force to be reckoned with in the Norwich economy.

Opposite the bank, under the sign of the Beehive, Alexander Thwaites, woollen and linen draper, mercer, hosier and hemp-cloth manufacturer had his establishment. In the spring of 1790 —and doubtless in subsequent years—Mr Thwaites went to London and returned with a large new and fashionable assortment of goods. Later in the year he had a large importation of Irish linens and French cambrics. Woodforde bought Russia towelling here at 8d a yard.[3]

Messrs Worthington and Ling kept another drapery shop in London Lane, visiting London and Manchester to select elegant, fashionable and cheap articles in prints, muslins and dimities.

There were several grocers in the lane. Joseph Woolford sold fine old Cheshire and double and single Gloster cheeses, spermaceti oil, muscadine and sultana raisins, figs, prunes, Brazil and other nuts. In season he advertised Seville oranges, China oranges and lemons which were remarkably high flavoured and would make excellent wine. James Hicks at

No 5 offered lump sugar at 11d a pound and Scotch snuff at
1½d an ounce. He stocked spices, blue, mustard, coffee, cocoa,
chocolate, teas and candles. Unlike Thomas Hawkins he seems
to have found a market for foreign starch—he advertised best
Poland starch at 7½d a pound. Woodforde tells us that Hicks
was a very stout man. One evening in June 1795 he had the
misfortune to share the London coach with him and three other
inside passengers but luckily, "we dropped the stout man at
Bury". Mr Hicks had commodious premisses. In 1793 he was
letting off rooms to Mr Immanuel from London who painted
portraits—likenesses guaranteed—from £1 1s od to £5 5s od.[4]
Before the end of the century Mr Hicks had given up and No 5
became a music shop under the direction of Joseph Hardingham
who also taught the German flute, fife, hobey, clarinet, horn,
trumpet, basoon, clario and serpent. He repaired instruments
and sold medals and coins, teas, coffee and chocolate. In 1797
he issued a token halfpenny with a view of the cathedral on one
side and a bust of Handel on the reverse, "payable by
Hardingham, musician".

At No 2 London Lane was the shop of Jeremiah Freeman
who offered the best modern prints at London prices and
would frame them in the new mode giving the most elegant
effect. Freeman manufactured pier and dressing glasses and
offered to enrich chimney-pieces with wood or composition
ornaments. He framed pictures for the Norwich artists and
was himself the subject of an early portrait by John Sell
Cotman.[5] There was a rival art shop at the other end of the lane
where W. C. Edwards set up as an engraver and drawing master.
He later published a set of his own engravings of Norfolk
portraits.

At No 6 Richard Beatniffe, a tory member of the Common
Council, kept his bookshop. When in 1790 he was elected
Sheriff he paid a fine of £80 to be excused from this duty for
ever. In 1795 he was advertising a stock of 6000 duodecimos in
various languages and a select collection of modern books in
plain and elegant bindings. He bought up libraries and when
hostilities did not prevent imported books from France, Italy
and Spain. He had a printing press from which he published
his *Norfolk Tour* or *Traveller's Pocket Companion*, compiled from

many folio and quarto volumes too large and expensive to be of use to a gentleman traveller. The *Tour* was popular enough to be reprinted a number of times over several decades. In 1790 Beatniffe informed his customers that Mr Wilkie of St Paul's Churchyard had obtained a licence for the sale of national lottery tickets at his shop "The delay, risk and expence of sending to London will be avoided and the security equal". Half tickets for the Irish lottery cost £3 18s od, for the English £8 10s od—the maximum prizes £10,000 and £20,000 respectively.[6]

London Lane had a sadler in George King who had invented an elastic saddle approved for its ease in not heating the rider. He had so perfected his invention as to be able to sell it at the same price as an ordinary saddle. He also supplied gentlemen's and servant's hunting caps, whips and belts and he manufactured and repaired umbrellas.

An important shop in the lane was that of John Sims, Chymist and Druggist. In 1795 Sims, himself a whig, took into partnership young John Pitchford who, as we have seen, was an extreme and active radical. They also had an Elaboratory in St Simon's where they made up oil of vitriol, spirits of salts, dyers mordants and other preparations to sell wholesale. Two years later Pitchford's involvement was limited to the wholesale business and this seems to have left him plenty of free time. Besides his political activities Augustus Hare tells us that in the summer of 1797 he was almost daily at Earlham reading, singing, walking, boating, and playing cricket with the Gurney girls and finishing up the evening with a dance. Hare quotes his journal with an account of how on Thursday 29 July he spent 17 hours with his "seven most enchanting friends" and tore himself away with difficulty.[7] Pitchford being a Roman Catholic John Gurney was prompted by the Friends to ask him to relax his visits and in due time the friendship cooled.

Near where London Lane narrowed to Cockey Lane, Edmund Cotman set up as a haberdasher and hosier towards the end of the century. It was probably here that his son, John Sell Cotman, painted his portrait, in a black coat with a white cravat, studying a bill.[8] Across the lane was the shop of John Theobald, breechesmaker and leather-seller. His trade was a skilled one for it was said that the tailors could not make breeches to fit as the breeches-makers did and the latter could charge twice as much as the tailors, John Theobald made periodic trips to London to buy leather and could supply breeches in buck, doe, grained oil, beaver or black leather. He was a very religious man and liked to take his part—perhaps more than his part—in the affairs of his church. When in 1791 he transferred his membership from the Old Meeting to St Mary's Baptist church Joseph Kinghorn, minister of the receiving church, wrote rather ruefully of it—"God having some awkward sheep in His fold". John Theobald considered that his religion exempted him from the need to worry about worldly events. During the invasion scares he would always counter any expression of alarm with the words, "The Lord reigneth, let the earth be glad". But there is no reason to suppose that his doe-skin breeches were not as he claimed "as neat as could be bought in London".

There were rival confectioners, pastry cooks and gingerbread-makers in Cockey Lane—Francis Horne at No 5 and John Nutter at No 15 who differed in their views about the conduct of business, particularly as to the traditional celebration of Twelfth Night. Nutter was wont to advertise that his shop would be elegantly decorated that night and illuminated after the London taste with every ornament that art or fancy could invent. Customers could have plum cakes from 1d to £1 1s od. Horne on the other hand let it be known that he would make no public show as there had been disagreeable accidents owing to the narrowness of the lane. The expenses that used to attend such a show would be taken off the price of his goods. Nutter countered these objections by adding to his announcement an undertaking that there would be a convenient passage through his shop so that no interruption could happen to ladies and gentlemen. Woodforde recorded buying a cheese-cake at Nutter's for 2d. Had he been aware of the politics of the rivals he would doubtless have supported Horne who was a supporter of the government whereas Nutter voted whig. [9]

Cockey Lane had at least three shops selling wearing apparel. Mary Sherrel had succeeded her mother as a milliner at No 11 and would go to London in May and bring back elegant summer fashions. She continued supplying her late mother's valuable medicines for a bad breast and she let lodgings to genteel families for assize week and the musical festival. Arthur Brown offered fashionable hats and hosiery and W. G. Graham manufactured ribbands and stocked rich Florentines, tiffanies, Persians, sarsnets and in winter furs, muffs, tippets and bosom friends. In July 1792 Woodforde and Nancy sheltered from the rain in his shop and spent 12s on a pair of black silk stockings.

From the Old Medicinal Warehouse at No 12 Cockey Lane came the weekly *Norwich Mercury*. Newspaper publishing offices customarily sold the medicaments advertised in the paper, hence the name of the establishment. In 1788 the paper was acquired by Richard Bacon and his son-in-law Yarrington. Bacon carried on business elsewhere in the city as a grocer, auctioneer, appraiser and brandy merchant and it seems that the paper was managed by Yarrington until 1794 when Bacon's son Richard McKenzie Bacon took charge of it at the age of 18. At that time the paper sold for 4d, in 1797 the price was raised to 6d. The Old Medicinal Warehouse also sold books and stationery and in this trade had a rival of its own making in Mrs Anne Bowen at No 4. In 1790 poor Mrs Bowen who, she claimed, had been liberally educated, was left a helpless female, destitute of friends and relations, suddenly deprived by death of an affectionate but insolvent husband, with a helpless infant to provide for and the melancholy expectation of another. The *Norwich Mercury* took up her cause and opened a sub-scription list. This was widely supported by benevolent citizens who raised upwards of £200 enabling Mrs Bowen to carry on the business of her late husband. She made good use of the opportunity and in due course offered not only stationery but an assortment of musical instruments, pianofortes to let, improving books and teas, coffee, chocolate, starch, blue, spices and sago.

From the dark narrows of Cockey Lane we emerge onto the Gentleman's Walk with its broad pavement fronting the Marketplace. At the corner was Benjamin Boardman's hat manufactory where, besides fashionable hats for the family could be bought for the servants livery hats not excelled for beauty and strength. John Oxley had a rival establishment a few doors away where Nancy Woodforde spent 23s on a black beaver hat with a purple cockade and band. A hat for Britton bought there in 1795 cost 19s.[10]

J. Clarke, another haberdasher on the Walk, who served funerals, dyed hats and made umbrellas, in 1794 issued a token coin with a muff and a boa on one side and on the reverse an umbrella, a hat, a glove and a stocking. He evidently considered his tokens an important recommendation for he had a ton of them coined.

In November 1791 J. Challis who had a shoe shop here was able to reduce his prices because of a fall in the cost of Spanish leather. He offered the best bespoke pumps at 5s 6d, inferior pumps at 4s 6d and 4s and ladies' string clogs at 2s 3d.

At No 4 was P. J. Knights's shawl warehouse where could be seen the finest products of the Norwich looms. In 1791 the Society of Arts and Sciences awarded Mr Knights a medal for weaving a shawl-counterpane of silk and Spanish wool of fine texture four yards square without a seem, ornamented with flowers jointly by the loom and the needle. Two years later he exhibited his manufactures in New Bond St, London where his display was visited by the Queen and Princesses, whereafter he was proud to advertise as shawlmaker to the royal family. Mrs Coke also gave instructions to have part of her "elegant mansion" at Holkham fitted up with shawl-manufacture. At Christmas 1793 Knights was selling train-dresses from £2 2s 0d to £10 10s 0d and square shawls from 12s to £3 3s 0d. The shop window of Mr Knights's establishment was made in 1794 to the design of Mr Freeman and for taste and elegance "justly pronounced a masterpiece".

Further along the Walk was the shop of Dunham and Yallop whose double-fronted windows are depicted on a copper token halfpenny issued in 1792. The sign of an eagle stands over the door with "teas" engraved beneath it. Yet teas were not Dunham and Yallop's chief commodity—the edge inscription of the coin describes the business as goldsmiths. John Harrison Yallop started in trade as a harberdasher in 1789 with the help of a loan of £25 from the city. Not long after he and Dunham were advertising themselves as goldsmiths, haberdashers and cutlers. A buying trip to London in 1795 resulted in the offer of a large assortment of cornelian, gold and gilt earrings, silver and plated tea and coffee urns, Pontipool and Japanned trays, besides Derbyshire petrifactions for chimney ornaments. In 1796 the tour took in Birmingham and Sheffield as well as the metropolis and added a great variety of fishing-rods, leather trunks and pistols to the stock on offer.

Next to Dunham and Yallop's was the King's Head one of the city's principal inns and the venue of many tory meetings. Here Woodforde often dined, supped and slept and was occasionally kept awake by a noisy club meeting below.

Beyond the King's Head, John Cozens had his grocery in a gabled house with bow windows projecting into the Walk on either side of the door. He took over the business in 1789 at the age of twenty, trading on a modest scale at first and buying in part from other Norwich grocers. In 1791 he entered into partnership with his brother-in-law Jonathan Davey who probably introduced substantial capital.[11] Cozens's "Bought Book" records the purchase of hogsheads of "sope", puncheons of molasses, sperm oil and whale oil and chests of tea which were usually brought by sea from London. Other commodities he handled were cheeses—Wiltshire, Cheshire and Gloster—Mecklenburgh blue, Poland starch, tobacco and snuff, hops, spices, fruit and nuts, gunpowder, shot and candles. Sugar was by far the largest item of his trade, teas the second. Cozens's business increased steadily with a slight check in 1793, the first year of the war, up to 1796. 1797 we know was a bleak year and trade fell off, but from 1799 on there were regular increases. In 1801 his turnover was about £400 a week of which £100 was in cash sales, nearly half of them made on Saturdays. The money was paid into his account at Gurney's Bank. Both Cozens and Davey were extreme radicals. Years later Davey made a joke which would have been dangerous in the 1790s. He boasted his intention to make a hole in the King's Head. He purchased the neighbouring inn of that name, pulled it down, and created Davey Place, perhaps the first "foot street" in Norwich.

Further down the Gentleman's Walk was the woollen and linen drapery of John Toll & Co., whence the Gurney girls

watched the election in 1796. Next door to Toll, Thomas
Bignold purveyed brandy, wine and hops. He was also an
enthusiast for insurance and in 1792 was largely responsible for
the foundation of the Norfolk and Norwich General Assurance
Company, which raised £100,000 in shares of £200 each and
offered protection against losses by fire. Four trustees and
eighteen directors were appointed including three Harveys and
three Gurneys. To ensure the success of the venture both sides
of political opinion were well represented. Bignold himself
was secretary and issued policies from his shop. The new
company was in competition with the London offices. The
Royal Exchange Assurance and the Phoenix and the Sun Fire
Offices, for example, had agents here and advertised in the
Norwich newspapers. Its operations seem to have given satisfaction. A case in point was the fire at Thomas Mark's starch
office in December 1793. Through the exertions of the public
and the timely arrival of St Clement's parish fire-engine the
fury of the flames was abated and in three hours extinguished.
The *Norwich Mercury* commented on the kind and ready attendance of a committee of the directors of the insurance office
and their ready acquiescence in discharging the amount of the
estimate of damage. In 1795 the company had 47 agents over
East Anglia and was offering to insure all live and dead farm
stock for 3s per cent. By 1797 premium income was £3500 a
year and the amount insured nearly £2,500,000 but at this point
Thomas Bignold quarrelled with the Board who dismissed him
and transferred their operations to the office of Adam Taylor,
an attorney, in St Giles'. Bignold, not to be deterred, found 28
friends who subscribed to the "Norwich Union Society for
Insuring against Loss by Fire". The very large profits made by
insurance companies had, he said, induced a number of persons
in the city and neighbourhood to form a society for insuring
each other for the sole benefit of the persons insured. The
premium which in other offices was applied to the profit of a
few individuals was here only deposited to make good losses
and charges, it being all returned (except what was applied to
those purposes) in proportion to the amount of each person's
insurance.[12] Thomas Bignold's new venture was a radical
innovation which evidently appealed to the supporters of the

Revolution. John Cozens and Jonathan Davey were among his original directors and all the others whose politics can be traced were blue-and-white voters. His persistence was rewarded; in the long run his Norwich Union Society was to absorb the older company.

Nearby Bignold's establishment W. T. Robberds kept a stationery warehouse, where, his advertisements told, he always had stocks of the best writing foolscaps, being part-proprietor of the Swanton paper mill. He ran a circulating library with all the most approved publications and offered insurance against militia service.[13]

Also on the Gentleman's Walk was Gardiner's print shop where one could have taken a perfect likeness in minature profile for 2s 6d. Here ladies could take lessons in painting on silk—£2 2s od for three—or on glass—£1 1s od for two lessons.

At the corner of White Lion Lane, where the Walk ended and the Haymarket began, was James Critchfield's cutlery shop where Woodforde was wont to buy razors "warrented good".[14]

The Haymarket had nearly a score of shops selling clothes, brushes, baskets, cheese, china and other commodities. John Buckle who was Mayor in 1793 had an ironmongery here. The turpentine and pitch he stored in the cellar caused anxiety when a fire broke out there in 1796 but the ready exertions of all ranks of the people and the timely assistance of the military got it under without considerable damage. Thomas Back's grocery business nearby later went over to the wine trade but retained the family name down to the 1960s. Amyot and Bennet made and repaired clocks, watches and jacks for the kitchen fire. Peter Amyot's clocks may sometimes still be seen in Norfolk houses. Though himself a tory he articled his son Thomas to the radical attorneys Foster and Unthank. Young Thomas stuck to his father's politics and in the 1802 election acted as agent for Windham, afterwards going to London as his private secretary. He became an enthusiastic antiquary and one of the founders of the Camden Society.[15]

For an "Upholder's" shop we must turn down White Lion Lane to the warehouse of Edward Crane. Crane was wont to make summer journeys to London, coming back, as his advertisements would tell, with an elegant assortment of every article in the upholstery, paper-hanging and carpet branches. He had papers in the newest patterns from 2s 6d to $2\frac{1}{2}$d a yard, painted and mahogany chairs, Brussels, Wilton and Cirencester carpets, blankets, quilts and counterpains.[16]

From all this it is apparent that Norwich could provide all that was required for a comfortable life for those who could afford it. For many of the citizens there can have been little opportunity to shop beyond buying the necessities of life. Perhaps it is not surprising that, though there were none of the opportunities afforded by the modern supermarket, the crime of shop-lifting was pretty common. At the Assizes in 1791 two Blofield girls were found guilty of a shop-lifting foray. They had stolen two women's beaver hats from Oxley's shop on the Walk; six yards of "linen cheque" from John Browne's besides books and cards from Mr Stephenson's where they had gone ostensibly to buy a child's book. They were sentenced to six months hard labour and solitary confinement in the Bridewell. This was a lenient sentence; others on similar charges were sentenced to seven years transportation and went to help populate Australia. As the *Chronicle* reporter said, "Frequent instances of shoplifting in this city require the utmost vigilance".

REFERENCES

1. Woodforde, vol. IV, pp. 17, 35.
2. Woodforde, vol. V, p. 174.
3. Woodforde, vol. III, pp. 269, 302.
4. Woodforde, vol. IV, p. 208. *Norwich Mercury*, 6 July 1793, 30 May 1795.
5. S. D. Kitson, *Life of John Sell Cotman*, p. 105.
6. *Norwich Mercury*, 6 Nov. 1790.
7. A. J. C. Hare, *Gurneys of Earlham*, vol. I, p. 83.
8. S. D. Kitson, op. cit., pp. 4, 106.
9. Woodforde, vol. III, 262.
10. Woodforde, vol. IV, pp. 30, 207, 287.
11. Copeman's of Norwich.
12. *Norwich Mercury*, 21 Mar. 1795, 25 Feb. 1797, 25 Mar. 1797.
13. *Norwich Mercury*, 25 Sept. 1790.
14. Woodforde, vol. III, pp. 95, 110, vol. IV, p. 19.
15. D.N.B.
16. *Norwich Mercury*, 12 June 1790.

10 *The Service of Health*

At the end of the eighteenth century there were some 24 doctors—physicians and surgeons—practising in Norwich. They cared for the health not only of the citizens but of those who dwelt in the country round. We read in Woodforde's diary of Norwich doctors being called to Weston House and to other country patients. When the parson himself was ill Nancy sent for Dr Lubbock and paid a fee of £3 3s od for his advice, which Woodforde later refunded though he could remember nothing of the visit.[1]

The well-to-do would be treated in their homes—even down to the present century surgery was carried out at home. The Norfolk and Norwich Hospital, founded in 1772, with some 90 beds was strictly a charity. It received only patients recommended by subscribers as being devoid of means to pay for their treatment. Some were sent by the Guardians of the Poor from country districts. When soldiers were treated the army paid the bill—in 1790 at 6d a day. Casualties were admitted from accidents but if they were found able to pay were required to do so—a fee of £3 3s od to the surgeon and 1s a day subsistence was demanded of a case in 1797. The honorary staff consisted of four physicians, three surgeons and three assistant surgeons. The physicians and principal surgeons were each allowed to have two pupils under instruction. There were two nurses receiving £7 7s od a year and seven more at £6 6s od. The matron's salary was £15.

In 1797 there was talk of dissecting bodies in the hospital. The Board then ruled that no malefactors should be brought in for dissection without the written consent of the majority of physicians and surgeons.[2] Apart from malefactors post mortem dissections sometimes took place. In 1802 John Beckwith, the organist of St Peter's Mancroft, witnessed one in which many curious particulars were brought to light. He described the incident at a meeting of the United Friars Society and Edward Colman the surgeon elucidated what he told them. Beckwith was evidently interested in the functions of the human body. He had on an earlier occasion read to the Society "a very pleasant and ingenious dialogue between the intestines, each of which was personified; explaining in a professional manner their physical properties".[3]

The doctors' pupils, according to the custom of the times, would live in the houses of their masters and as might be expected they indulged in occasional pranks. Dr Rigby at his house in St Giles' besides his family, pupils and servants had young John Crome as a resident errand boy. Crome used to relate how on one occasion a patient required to be bled and how, the doctor being absent, he undertook the operation with such effect that the life of the sufferer was almost sacrificed. The tale was probably apocryphal but Crome who was only about 13 at the time made himself sufficiently felt in the household for the doctor's pupils to play a practical joke on him. They took the skeleton from the surgery and placed it in his bed. Crome, highly incensed, took the skeleton by the vertebrae of the neck and hurled it down the well of the staircase to the hall below.[4]

The hospital was governed by a committee of subscribers and every week two house visitors were appointed from the governors living in or near the city. They were supposed to walk through the wards with white wands in their hands inquiring of the patients whether they had been treated according to the rules, and of the staff as to the behaviour of the patients. Such a visit is described by Woodforde on 2 April 1789:

Before Tea I walked to the Norfalk and Norwich Hospital with Mr Priest who is one of the Visitors for this Week, and we walked over almost the whole Hospital into almost every Ward, and I think I never saw an Hospital kept in a better and more clean, airy manner. All the poor Creatures in it appeared quite cheerful and grateful in their present Complaints. I saw there a Stone that was taken out of a man by Mr Donne, and the Man now living,

of a most extraordinary Nature, called the Mulberry Stone
the Colour and make of the Mulberry, but very large.
The poor man was a long time under the Operation.[5]

Despite the dread that surgery must have inspired in the
days before anaesthetics, William Donne during his thirty
years on the hospital staff (1771–1804) performed no less than
173 lithotomies with a mortality of one in seven, while Philip
Meadows Martineau, his apprentice who went on to study at
Edinburgh, London, Paris and Geneva and rejoined him as a
partner in 1777, performed 149, gaining an European reputation for his version which became known as "the Norwich
operation for Stone".[6]

Apart from doctor's prescriptions numerous medicaments
were available to those who could afford them. Judging by the
amount of advertising space used they must have been very
popular with the readership of the newspapers. These con-
coctions claimed to cure most of the ills that flesh is heir to.
Sufferers from stomach pains could rely on Magnetic Effluvia
recommended by the wife of a gauze-weaver between Brazen
Gates and Ber St Gates who was cured by three applications
after enduring two months of affliction. Or they might resort
to Scot's Pills, which had had 100 years of proof. They were
also good for dropsical complaints, indigestion after hard
drinking, surfeits, want of appetite or sleep, rheumatism,
gravel and all obstructions with the added advantage that
"worms cannot breed in the bodies of those who frequently
take this medicine". Another alternative was Hunter's Restorative Balsam for nervous disorders and inward decays, especially
those arising from the immoderate use of tea. True Daffy's
Elixir was recommended for stone, gravel, ulcerated kidneys,
gout, rheumatism, cholic, phthisic, dropsy, scurvy, surfeits,
convulsions, disorders of women and children, consumptions,
piles, fevers, agues, fluxes, spitting blood and pains in the
breast, limbs and joints while Betton's True British Oil was
nearly as wide in its application besides being "infallible for
certain diseases of cattle". Dr Steer's Opodeldoc was universally
acknowledged efficient in rheumatism, lumbago, bruises,
sprains and cramp. It was excellent for burns, scalds and the

sting of venomous insects and the best embrocation for horses wrung in the withers or galled with the saddle.

Leake's Pillula Salutaria might be expected to cure venereal diseases in fifteen days but if it failed "the patient has the happy assurance that he is at the eve of being so restored, let the degree of malignancy be ever so great". Dr Hodson offered his Persian Restorative for that weakness and debility which people bring upon themselves by an imprudent habit too common among youths in great schools who thus find themselves disgusted at the very thought of pleasure, lost in company, and sometimes plunged into the deepest melancholy. Cephalic snuff would cure headache, restore memory and protect against infections when visiting the sick while Devonshire Tooth Tincture immediately relieved violent toothache, fastened loose teeth, prevented decay and rendered the breath delicately sweet.

There seems to have been no dentist resident in the city though visiting dentists were sometimes available. In October 1790 Mr and Mrs Sedman took rooms in St Michael's at Plea. They informed the nobility, gentry and public in general that Mr Sedman had invented a safe way of fitting artificial teeth which were an ornament to the mouth. Charges were 5s for cleaning; 5s for stuffing with gold; 10s 6d for an artificial tooth and for a whole set £21. Other dentists came from time to time. In May 1797 Z. Florance from London was at the Wounded Hart in St Peter's advertising himself as a dentist and operator on corns. His services included scaling and cleaning teeth and transplanting them; setting artificial teeth and filling hollow teeth with gold, silver or lead. He would wait upon ladies and gentlemen in their own houses. Joseph Kinghorn, who had evidently not availed himself of Florance's services, wrote to his father in October 1797:

> I observe what you say about the Toothache. I have been troubled with it lately but my tooth is very hollow. I am obliged to keep mine constantly filled with a piece of ginger which swells and excludes the air. If notwithstanding that it will be painfull a bit of opium or opium mixed with camorph only about the size of a pins head quiets it &

will keep it quiet a day or two. This I put into the tooth &
a piece of ginger at the top as a cork.

Of all Norwich medicos, in William Taylor's estimation,
Philip Meadows Martineau had the most profitable practice.
Taylor arranged for Henry Southey to be apprenticed to him
and wrote to his brother Robert that Martineau's weight of
character, moral and professional, was calculated to preserve
the esteem and his urbanity to conciliate the love of his appren-
tices.[7] Woodforde often mentions his services to the Custances.
He recounts too how when Nancy was staying at the Corbould's
house in St Giles', Martineau was sent for because the servant
maid was "taken in labour and soon miscarried, which she
denied to the last". The doctor soon came and "things were
made more easy".[8] Martineau was active in many fields of
Norwich life. He had been the originator (in 1784) of the
public subscription Library. Later he was to play a leading part
in establishing the triennial musical festival to raise funds for
the hospital. In religion Martineau was a member of the
Unitarian congregation at the Octagon chapel and in politics
like the majority of the Norwich doctors as he was a whig and a
consistent blue and white voter though his partner William
Donne was of the other persuasion. The author of his memoir
tells us that he was censured for his unremitting love of society,
but "in one exposed continually to the chambers of misery and
pain the mind becomes unfitted for thoughtful pursuits and to
revive the exhausted powers it is almost necessary to turn to
scenes of cheerfulness and ease".

Martineau built Bracondale Woods on sloping ground
towards Trowse, recently demolished to make way for the
headquarters of the Norfolk County Council which still benefits from his tree-planting.

James Alderson, brother of Robert who started his career as
minister of the Octagon chapel and later became Recorder of
Norwich, was another doctor of considerable reputation. Among
his patients was Joseph Kinghorn who describes the doctor-
patient relationship in a letter to his father in January 1797:

> Since I wrote last I have been a few days ill but thro
> Mercy I am restored pretty well tho not quite. I could not

preach Jan. 1 & only once on the 8th. The complaint I
was told by my Doctor was indigestion it came on with
pain in the head & feverishness & I was apprehensive it
would prove a fever. The Dr said no it was nothing
serious—he gave me Castor Oil to cleanse the bowels wc
he said was the principal thing wanted. . . . The Gentleman
who attended me is the son of a Dissenting Minister—he
himself is an Infidel—yet he would take no fees of me
saying I will never fleece the flock of Christ— . . . and tho
he attended me every day—he literally ran away when I
thanked him & would not hear me. . . . I told him of your
case [David Kinghorn had complained of a sore cold and
cough] . . . He said he saw nothing in it to be afraid of.
Opening medicines he said would hurt you because they
weakened. He thought it likely 15 or 20 drops of
Laudanum would be of use. Tho I think this likely yet
perhaps 10 would do better as they might probably disorder your head. . . . I esteem it a mercy that I have a man
of ability at hand who so cheerfully attends in affliction—
for when I had a cold . . . he chid me in the street because
I did not tell him and take his advice.

Apart from his private practice we are told that the forms in
the large hall of Dr Alderson's house in Colegate—where the
Norvic Shoe Factory now stands—were full every morning
from 8.30 to 11.00 when he freely prescribed for some 400 to
500 people weekly.[9] In September 1800 he announced that
vaccinations were taking up too much of the time he employed
in giving advice to the poor and he had arranged a free vaccination service for "the lower classes of the people" at the surgery
of W. F. Rand in Samson and Hercules Court.

Other doctors doubtless ministered to the poor among them
surely John Manning whose memorial in St Stephen's church
tells us that his great beneficence was not so much a sacrifice to
duty as the offspring of a feeling heart which extended to the
whole animal creation. In 1795 the United Friars Society
commended the humanity of the surgeons Aldhouse and
Johnson in not only gratuitously affording medical aid to two
poor families but providing them with nourishment as well.

Apart from the private benevolence of the doctors the Court of Guardians employed two Surgeons at a salary of £50 a year each to attend the poor in the city's workhouses—generally 1200 to 1300 of them—and to act as man-midwives in specified areas. In 1801 the salaries were raised to £60 per annum. Another surgeon received £30 a year to look after the aged in the Great Hospital and Doughty's Hospital and the young in the Boys' and Girls' Hospitals. When they deemed it necessary the authorities were prepared to spend additional sums on the care of the health of those in their charge. In the spring of 1800 the guardians called in Dr Lubbock to deal with what they described as "a malignant fever" and he refered to as "an epidemic". They thanked him for his unwearied attendance and important services and voted a fee of £25 which he refused saying that he felt it a duty to join his efforts with theirs to promote the welfare and safety of the poor.

Those in charge of the various institutions were responsible for the hygiene of the inmates. The master of the Great Hospital was specifically charged to take care that every part of it and the beds and furniture were kept clean. He seems to have had difficulty in complying with this requirement for on several occasions James Brunton, one of the Mace Officers to the Mayor, had to be brought in to clean the beds and kill the bugs.[10]

The mentally sick were cared for at the Bethel Hospital founded earlier in the century "for the relief and assistance of poor lunatics", where they were under the direction of Drs Beevor and Manning and of James Keymer, one of the city surgeons. Amelia Opie, Dr Alderson's daughter, told how, in her childhood, the lunatics would come to the windows of the Bethel to beg for halfpence to buy snuff; how she one day attracted the attention of a man called Goodings who begged her to throw a coin over the door in the wall of the exercise yard and of her alarm at hearing the clanking of his chain as he came to retrieve it. Goodings admired the nosegay she wore, whereafter she often spent her pocker-money on flowers for him. Later on with two gentlemen friends Amelia visited the interior of the Bethel where she saw among others "a poor girl just arrived whose hair was not yet cut off". These remarks tell something of the treatment of lunatics in those days.[11]

One of the masters of the Bethel, James Bullard, appointed in 1798 was later murdered by a patient. Sometimes the Guardians thought it desirable to send to the Bethel one of their charges "being insane and unable to support himself". In such case he (or she) would be certified by the city surgeons to be free of infectious disease and the master of the workhouse would be charged to see that he was provided with clean and proper apparel.[12] Lunatics who were able to pay for their keep could be placed in a house at Lakenham where Dr Rigby had a licence to keep ten.[13]

Some doctors found time to take a large part in the life of the city. Edward Rigby was one of the most active citizens in political and civic affairs, yet he was also prominent in his profession, performing 106 operations for the stone at the hospital between 1790 and 1814, writing professional works and introducing vaccination to the city. His *Essay on the Uterine Haemorrhage* was translated into French and German and ran into six English editions.[14] Edward Colman, Assistant Surgeon at the Hospital from 1790, served as Sheriff in 1795. Four years later he was Abbot of the United Friars Society and he was a frequent contributor to their discussions.

Dr John Beevor on the other hand, having been elected Sheriff in 1789 refused either to take the oath or to buy himself out by the customary fine. The Town Clerk sought legal advice and was told that the Court of King's Bench took the view that it was improper to call upon a practising physician whose immediate attendance and advice might at any time be necessary to individuals.[15]

Matters of hygiene were generally left to the individual. Public baths were available in Chapel Field. The charges in 1789 were 5s for the hot bath; 2s 6d for the tepid and 1s for the cold. A season ticket cost 21s for a year. These prices included the attendance and assistance of proper persons to the bathers of both sexes and the use of commodious dressing rooms warmed by good fires. William Taylor was wont to bathe almost daily at all seasons in the river at a bath house constructed in the stream near its entrance to the city.[16] He could scarcely have used any lower part of the stream for it was the receptacle of the city's refuse and remained so until sewage works were undertaken in the 1860s. Some people went to Yarmouth or Cromer to bathe in the sea for their health but the doctors were divided as to the efficacy of the practice. When Joseph Kinghorn was taken ill while on a visit to Yorkshire, his friend W. W. Wilkin went to consult Dr Beevor on his behalf who absolutely forbade sea bathing. Despite this Kinghorn on other advice "went into the sea" and felt comfortable after it.

As well as the services of doctors resident in the city there were occasional visits from travelling healers. Dr Graham, a notorious quack, came in June 1793 "en route from Lisbon and London to his house at Edinburgh" and demonstrated his earth bath, for the cure of diseases, weaknesses, wounds, ulcers, contractions, tremblings and lameness, in the garden of a cabinetmaker in St John's Maddermarket. The demonstration apparently consisted in burying himself up to the neck and remaining in that position some hours.[17] But the most notable visiting physician was the German, Dr Brodum. In the summer of 1789 he was in Somerset where he happened to meet with parson Woodforde on a visit to his relations. They went together to see the royal family at Sherborne.[18] Perhaps this chance meeting directed the doctor's thoughts to Norfolk. He came to Lynn in January 1791 and moved on to Norwich in March, taking rooms at John Gardiner's Print Shop in the market place and advertising successful cures accomplished at Lynn. The cure of Ann Mitchley who for eight years had been afflicted with a complaint which took away her sight and caused her finger joints to fly out in great knots was used as a stock advertisement for some years.

Dr Brodum recognised that it was unusual for the Faculty in England to advertise their cures, "But why", he asked, "should the afflicted suffer for a form?" His object was he said that the world might be acquainted where to fly for relief. Whatever skill he may have had in healing, he was certainly ahead of his time in the arts of advertising. His advice and medicines were offered gratis to the poor who could see him on Fridays and Saturdays between 9.00 and 12 o'clock or in the evening from 8.00 to 9.00. From those who came after midday he expected a fee of 10s 6d; for consultations by letter 21s. He must see those with cancers or wounds; for inward disorders it was enough to send their urine. Brodum visited Norwich again in 1793 and briefly in 1797 and apart from his visits kept up his contact by frequent advertisements in the local papers. He offered two medicines—the Botanical Syrup for scurvy, leprosy and scrophulous complaints and the Nervous and Restorative Cordial for the nervous, consumptive and deaf. Bottles of either could be had for 5s 4d, 11s 6d or 21s. In his advertisements he rang the changes between the two panaceas. He loved to beguile his readers with stories of the triumphs of his remedies over other forms of treatment. Perhaps the most notable was the case of Lady M, cured of a cancerous evil by the Botanical Syrup. Before taking it she had tried a trip to Bengal and the advice of the medicos of Weymouth, Bath, Harrogate and Scarborough to no avail.

In due course Dr Brodum was able to publish an extract from the *Gazette* of 10 April 1799 to the effect that His Majesty had been graciously pleased to grant him Royal Letters Patent for his valuable medicines. No doubt this rendered his cures even more popular than before.

REFERENCES

1. Woodforde, vol. V, p. 57.
2. Sir Peter Eade, *N. & N. Hospital*, p. 60.
3. Transactions of United Friars, 19 Oct. 1795.
4. MSS additions to Dawson Turner's Memoir of John Crome.
5. Woodforde, vol. III, p. 95.
6. A. Batty Shaw, N. & N. Hospital Lives of the Medical Staff.
7. J. W. Robberds, *Memoir of Wm. Taylor*, p. 365.
8. Woodforde, vol. IV, p. 196.
9. C. L. Brightwell, *Life of Amelia Opie*, p. 3.
10. Norwich Corporation Hospital Committee Minutes.
11. C. L. Brightwell, op. cit., pp. 14–16.
12. Guardians of the Poor Court Book.
13. Quarter Sessions book.
14. A. Batty Shaw, op. cit., p. 24.
15. Court of Mayoralty Book.
16. J. W. Robberds, op. cit., vol. II, p. 60.
17. R. J. Mackintosh, *Memoirs of Sir James Mackintosh*, p. 28.
18. Woodforde, vol. III, p. 127.

11 *Religious Affiliations*

Infidelity, as we have seen, was popular with some of the rising generation. As the Bishop of Norwich, preaching before the Lords on the appointed Fast Day in 1794 said:

> There is something extremely flattering to an ardent mind in the opposition to inveterate opinions. Scepticism is . . . better calculated for the display of a brilliant imagination, than a sober . . . consent with the established Faith.

Yet the doubters represented a small minority. Most of the population, whether from conviction or interest or mere habit maintained some link with the Church or with Dissent.

There were some forty clergymen of the established church living in the city including the dozen or so who inhabited the Close. Many of them held benefices elsewhere while some city churches were dependent on the ministrations of parsons from the country. The Rev. John Day lived at Horsford but came in fortnightly to take a service at St Benedict's where he held the perpetual curacy. The Rev. William Walford, rector of St Clement's, resided at Long Stratton and employed a curate at £30 a year, whereas the Rev. John Deacon, who actually lived in St Clement's was rector of Carleton St Mary's and also held fortnightly services in the Norwich churches of St Etheldreda and St Peter Southgate.

When Wesley visited Norwich in October 1790, he recorded:

> . . . we went to our own parish church, although there was no sermon there, nor at any of the 36 churches in the town, save the Cathedral and St Peter's.[1]

St Peter Mancroft was the wealthiest and best provided church in the city. The incumbent, the Rev. John Peele was resident in the parish though he also held two benefices in west Norfolk. The parish paid him a stipend of £100 a year—

raised in 1801 to £125. A second minister was paid £50 and a third, described as "reader of the weekly prayers", £26 a year. Few Norwich curates received more than £25 and so the second minister's place at St Peter's was an attractive one. When it fell vacant in 1791 by the death of Dr Harrington, who had been at the same time a Prebendary of Bath and Wells and held a benefice in Norfolk and another in Suffolk, there was no less than ten candidates for the post. The appointment was in the hands of the parishioners who decided to hold an election after the candidates had preached their second "approbation Sermon". It was agreed that there should be a ballot first of all ten and then a second ballot between the two who headed the first. The election was managed by two attornies, Samuel Harmer and William Unthank who hired rooms at the Angel for the purpose. The Rev. C. J. Chapman who had been second in the first ballot won the second with 128 votes to 104. The proceedings cost the parish almost £14.[2]

According to the answers to the Bishop's Visitation questions in 1801 there were some twenty churches in the city holding services every Sunday: others had a fortnightly service. In most the sacrament was observed four times a year though at St Andrew's, St Michael's at Plea, St Peter's Mancroft and St Stephen's there were monthly celebrations.

At the 1801 Visitation the Rev. Thomas Wigg Hancock of St Michael's at Plea complained that the four churches he was responsible for produced an income short of £100 per annum, while the Rev. Lancaster Adkin of St Andrew's said it was a general complaint of his brethren that their subsistance was scanty and precarious. While expenses increased collections at St Andrew's went down and then only amounted to £40 a year, a fact which he attributed to the anti-government sentiments, religious indifference and downright infidelity of too many of his parishioners.

St Peter's Mancroft boasted what was described in the inventory as a "beautiful organ", a rarity in parish churches at that date. The organist—John Beckwith succeeded his father Edward in 1794—had a salary of £30 a year, a sum as large as the total yearly disbursements of the smaller Norwich parishes. In 1799 the organ was found to be out of order. The par-

ishioners collected £95 to mend it and made a contract with Mr
Crotch to keep it in order for £6 6s od a year. In 1801 they
engaged three men at 20s each a quarter as "singers to the
organ" and four boys at 2s 6d a quarter.

An organ was something of a status symbol so it is not
surprising that after the Octagon Chapel had installed one in
1801 the neighbouring church of St George Colegate should
aspire to have an instrument in the next year. The parishioners
determined to buy an organ by public subscription and to rate
the parish for the organist's salary of £10 a year—the Octagon
paid £20. There was murmuring in some quarters at the thought
of this additional burden on the parish and so the subscribers
agreed to raise the salary as well. The organ was opened in
April 1802 with a grand concert when Beckwith played on it
with the support of a band of 90 preformers. 3s tickets for the
performance were taken up by an audience of 700.

The leaders of the tory party, the Harveys and Pattesons,
were Anglicans but not all members of the Established Church
were tories. The radical Dr Rigby was a churchman and some-
time churchwarden of St Giles' where he lived. In St Clement's
the Ives family who despite their intermarriage with the
Harvey's were whigs and were leading supporters of the
church. There was a Sunday school here and every new year's
day Alderman Ives regaled its 50 children with a dinner of
roast beef and plum pudding.[3] The school evidently taught
reading and writing for the churchwardens' accounts record
purchases of spelling books and writing books.

As regards the Dissenters the most important in the social
scale belonged to the "Presbyterian" congregation at the
Octagon Chapel where socinian or unitarian doctrine held sway.
The law which threatened those who denied the doctrine of
the Trinity with outlawry and death was a dead letter but to
enjoy the protection of the Toleration Act the Octagon
ministers had to subscribe to the doctrinal articles of the
Church of England—perhaps this was no more difficult for
them than it was for many Anglican clergy. Nationally the
Presbyterians were notable for political preaching. A sermon
by Dr Price, one of their leading ministers, had sparked off
Burke's "Reflections on the French Revolution". In Birming-

ham Dr Priestley's support of the Revolution had caused a violent reaction. But the Octagon ministers, Dr Enfield and the Rev. Pendlebury Houghton, though it was well known on which side their sympathies lay, seem to have been content to leave active participation in politics to the laymen of their congregation. Of Dr Enfield, who died in his prime in 1797 it was said he brought together men of opposite opinions and taught them to discuss with temper and urbanity their points of difference, to think that others may be honest and sincere as well as themselves and to prefer the advance of truth to the triumph of party.[4] Similarly the Rev. Pendlebury Houghton was reputed to be unable to feel the importance of many questions that divided the Christian world. He avoided controversial subjects and his eloquence, his countenance, voice and gesture secured an absolute command over the attention of his audience.[5] When he preached at the Octagon in 1801 in aid of the Norfolk and Norwich Hospital the collection was no less than £86 6s 9d.

To the Octagon congregation belonged most of the principal whig families in the city—the William Taylors and John Taylors (unrelated one to the other), the Marsh family (the carriers), several leading medical families, the Aldersons, Dalrymples and Martineaus, besides Alderman Elias Norgate, and Alderman John Green Basely, the Bolingbrokes, some of the Barnards and J. E. Smith the botanist.

Next door to the Octagon the Rev. Samuel Newton ruled the Independant Church at the Old Meeting. Newton was a veteran who had come to Norwich in 1757 to assist his father-in-law Dr Wood and had succeeded to the pastorate on his death ten years later. He had been tutor to William Godwin who complained of his strictness. Godwin in the introduction to his *Political Justice* said that he conceived politics to be the proper vehicle of a liberal morality. Possibly he formed this view in reaction against Newton, who seems not to have taken an active part in political affairs. John Barnard and Edward Barrow were members of his church as was William Youngman, a contributor to *The Cabinet*.

The Baptist Meeting House where Joseph Kinghorn ministered was in the neighbouring parish of St Mary's. As we have seen Kinghorn, though a supporter of liberal views, did not think it proper to express them in the pulpit. He was deeply interested in speculation as to how far Biblical prophecy was being fulfilled by the catastrophic events of his time. His congregation included a number of active radicals, among them Thomas Hawkins, who was his right hand man in church affairs, W. W. Wilkin his personal friend, and George Watson the miller of Saxlingham. There were also members like John Theobald who eschewed the politics of this world altogether.

Two other Baptist churches need to be mentioned—St Paul's and St Margaret's—called after the parishes in which they were situated. St Paul's was of Methodist origin. The Rev. Mark Wilks, trained at the Countess of Huntingdon's college at Trevecca, was sent to Norwich in 1776 to preach at the Tabernacle. Two years later he married and consequently, in accordance with the rules of the autocratic Countess, was dismissed from his post. Some years earlier the Rev. Thomas Bowman the evangelical vicar of Martham, impressed by the godlessness of the Norwich poor, had built a preaching house in St Paul's with a fine disregard for the parish clergyman.[6] This was now vacant and some of Wilks's Tabernacle congregation bought it and invited him to continue his ministry there. When he adopted Baptist tenets much of his congregation followed him in so doing but it was plain that those who stayed with him could not pay him a living wage. The larger congregation at St Mary's paid Kinghorn £60 a year in 1790 and gradually increased his salary till it reached £100 in the first year of the new century. Besides this he was able to add £21 to his income by tutoring three pupils. Wilks rectified his position by renting a farm at Heigham just outside the city. In 1790 he also offered himself for the post of Coroner but he claimed no more qualification for the appointment than the fact of having eight small children to support it is not surprising that he failed to secure it.[7] We have seen how great political activity he put forth. The good Countess may well have turned in her grave at having trained such a revolutionary. Among the members of Wilks's church John Cozens and Jonathan Davey were very active radicals and Charles Lawson a dyer was reported by Mr Alderton in 1792 to be a member of the club at the Bell Inn.

Samuel Fisher, pastor of St Margaret's Baptist church took quite the opposite view of the situation to Wilks and was a consistent supporter of the government. He wrote against William Richards the Baptist minister of Lynn who favoured the French and published in 1794 a sermon on "The duty of Subjects to the Civil Magistrate" for which he was said to have received the thanks of the Prime Minister. Perhaps the clue to his divergence from the views of his fellow denominationalists lay in his own sad history. He had come from Nottingham in 1762 to minister to the St Mary's congregation. For some years his ministry was popular and numbers increased but then he was accused of a grave moral lapse. The majority of the church found the case against him proved and excommunicated him but a few who believed in him built him a little chapel in Pottergate where he ministered for the rest of his life, holding for some years simultaneously the pastorate of a church at Wisbech. [8]

Apart from the Gurney family Norwich Quakers did not at this period appear much in the public eye. But there was always a hearing for a gifted preacher as was evidenced by the visit of the American Friend William Savery in February 1798. His part in the conversion of Elizabeth Gurney (afterwards Mrs Fry) is too well known to need repetition but the public impact of his visit is of interest. According to the *Norfolk Chronicle* he commanded the attention of a crowded and respectable audience of nearly 2000—surely an exaggeration of numbers! —at the Friends meeting house on Sunday evening for upwards of two hours. His subject was founded on the maxim that the society which did not revert to first principles was liable to decay. John Pitchford recorded:

In the evening I went to the Quakers' Meeting. As there was a great crowd and no room to sit down, I placed myself on the staircase, but Mr Joseph Gurney soon beckoned me thence and placed me among the preachers. . . . The name of the speaker was Savery, and his sermon the best I have ever heard among Quakers, so full of candour and liberality. My only objection to it was its excessive length—two hours and a half. [9]

Savery himself was rather shocked at the "gaiety" of Norwich Friends and noted that the marks of wealth and grandeur were too obvious.

The Methodists had been established in Norwich for a generation before our period, suffering persecution and occasioning riots at an earlier date. The two wings of the movement were represented by the Countess of Huntingdon's Tabernacle in St Martin's in the shadow of the Bishop's Palace wall and Wesley's Cherry Lane Chapel off Pitt St. The Norwich Methodists at this time seem not to have been greatly concerned with politics or the affairs of the world though they were doubtless alive to the needs of the poor among whom they ministered. Richard Reece, a young preacher, noted in his journal in March 1789 that the citizens expressed their joy at the King's recovery from illness by a general illumination and expressed the opinion that it would have been more Godly to expend the money in acts of beneficence.[10] Thomas Mendham of Briston, a prominent Norfolk Methodist, wrote a pamphlet which was published shortly after Tom Paine's "Rights of Man" and bore the same title. He urged contentment—although his readers might have scant meals, they were better off than poor African slaves. He enjoined submissiveness to superiors whose goodwill might be won by obliging them; and to enjoy what they earned, living in their cottages as secure as Princes in their palaces—"perhaps you do so now with more liberty than the King and Queen of France and their family enjoy". Mendham expostulated with the masters too, pointing out that their labourers could not eat as large a dumpling when meal was 20d a stone as when it was 12d. Either they should have their meal at 12d or their wages should be adequate to its price. In general Mendham attributed the ills of the times to too little religion, too much licentiousness, and high-flying ambition. As to the Revolution, the topic that constituted the rage of the day, he was content to leave it to Edmund Burke and Tom Paine and company to scuffle about. There could scarcely be more opposite outlooks than those of Mendham and Wilks, yet there was no rift between them on the religious front and Wilks would on occasion preach from Mendham's pulpit at Briston.[11]

The Roman Catholics also call for mention. Till as recently

as 1778 public worship had been forbidden them but they now had chapels in St John's Maddermarket and in St Swithin's and by 1801 a small settlement of nuns in St George's Colegate. One of their number, John Pitchford, was as we have seen an active radical: probably the majority were of the other political persuasion. Many were émigrés and presumably not favourably inclined to the Revolution which had driven them out of France. Joseph Kinghorn in a letter written in April 1795 tells how he attended worship at one of their chapels on Good Friday afternoon and heard a sermon on the infinite love of Christ—"One tear shed by such a being as the Son of God could have been sufficient to have washed away the sins of a world." Kinghorn thought the preacher reasoned away the plain language of his Bible and came to a conclusion nearly socinian—"Thus extremes may meet".

After Windham's volte face and his election as a tory War Minister in 1794, Mark Wilks twitted him with having found new friends in the precincts of the cathedral.[12] In truth the Close was a tory stronghold though four of the clerics there had voted for Windham in his blue and white days, no doubt on personal grounds. The intellectual attitude of Dissent inclined naturally to the blue and white side of politics; that induced by allegiance to the Established Church to the orange and purple. Yet despite these differences of political outlook there was no religious animosity at this time between Norwich Churchmen and Dissenters. The clergy in the 1801 Visitation reports where they mentioned Dissenters at all invariably referred to them as "quiet and orderly". The parish being a civil as well as an ecclesiastical entity nonconformists as well as anglicans took part in parish meetings and served in parish offices. Even in St Peter's Mancroft, the best conducted parish in the city, the Baptist Jonathan Davey attended a vestry meeting and agreed with his fellow parishioners on the appointment of a sexton, while the unitarian Alderman Norgate served for some years on the committee for auditing the church-wardens' accounts.

In St George's Colegate, a parish in which nonconformists were very numerous, William Barnard and John Taylor regularly attended vestry meetings and in 1797 Thomas Martineau was appointed churchwarden in the same year in which he was chosen to be a deacon of the Octagon congregation. He was followed next year as churchwarden by Martin Willement another Octagon member. John Sidel, a Quaker, was one of the overseers for this parish in 1798 and 1799, and in the latter year when the Bishop preached a charity sermon there in aid of the fund for restoring persons apparently drowned, John Taylor another Octagon deacon wrote three hyms for the occasion which were sung to the accompanyment of a respectable band of gentlemen and professional performers attending gratuitously. The congregation for this service was said to number a thousand and the collection raised £73 12s 9d. In the neighbouring parish of St Michael Coslany, Robert Kitton, a Baptist, was active in vestry affairs.

Though there was no apparent animosity on the lines of religious difference in parish meetings it should not be supposed that all was always sweetness and light. When the St Martin's at Oak parishioners were discussing the need for re-roofing their church, the clerk, evidently with deep feeling, entered in his book:

> There was one person whom seem to contradick every Proposal made but he was over ruled.

REFERENCES

1. *Journal of the Rev. John Wesley*, vol. IV, p. 485.
2. St Peter's Mancroft Parish Book.
3. *Norwich Mercury*, 2 Jan. 1790, 3 Jan. 1795.
4. J. W. Robberds, *Memoir of Wm. Taylor*, vol. I, p. 208.
5. J. G. Robberds, *Sermons of the late Pendlebury Houghton*, p. xvi, xxiii.
6. J. Browne, *History of Congregationalism in Norfolk and Suffolk*, p. 197.
7. *Norwich Mercury*, 18 Dec. 1790, 22 Jan. 1791.
8. E. Deacon, *Samuel Fisher*.
9. A. J. C. Hare, *Gurneys of Earlham*, vol. I, p. 97.
10. Diary of Rev. Richard Reece.
11. B. Cozens-Hardy, *Mary Hardy's Diary*, p. 120.
12. Mark Wilks, *Two Sermons on the Origins and Stability of the French Revolution*.

12 *Pursuits of the Mind*

"In the years preceding the French Revolution there was more mind afloat in Norwich than is usually found outside the literary circles of the metropolis."[1] So wrote J. W. Robberds the biographer of William Taylor the younger. William Taylor himself was the centre of the literary circle in the city. His father of the same name, a merchant engaged in the export of Norwich stuffs, sent him abroad to complete his education. After visiting the Netherlands, Geneva, France, Italy and Prussia and spending a year at Detmold in Germany, he came home in November 1782 at the age of seventeen to enter his father's business. Anxious to be free of the responsibilities of the counting-house he ultimately pursuaded his father to give up trading and to live on the proceeds of his capital. This was effected in 1791 whereafter, despite constant anxieties about the failure of his investments and the loss of his capital, he devoted himself entirely to literary pursuits. He was a diligent writer, translating from the German, versifying, reviewing books and writing articles for the *Monthly Review*, the *Monthly Magazine* and other publications. His subjects were wide-ranging, among them: "The Jews in England", "Songs of the Negroes of Madagascar", "Geology", "English Hexameters", and essays in biblical criticism and theology, besides "Historic Doubts concerning Joan of Arc" and an "Ode in Praise of Tea".

No one reads William Taylor's writings today. Indeed he developed a style which makes them somewhat hard to read. Sir James Mackintosh wrote of him: "He does not speak any other language but the Taylorian; but I am so fond of his vigour and originality that . . . I have studied and learned his language."

His friend and correspondent Robert Southey was even more explicit: ". . . you have ruined your style by Germanisms,

Latinisms and Greekisms, . . . you are sick of a surfeit of knowledge, . . . your learning breaks out like scabs and blotches upon a beautiful face." Southey goes on to say, "You taught me to write English by what you said of Burger's language and by what I felt from your translations". Taylor was widely read in his own day and exercised a considerable influence. J. G. Lockhart in his *Memoirs of Sir Walter Scott* recounts that Mrs Barbauld in the autumn of 1795 took to Edinburgh a manuscript copy of Taylor's then unpublished translation of Bürger's ballad "Ellenore" and read it at a party at Dugald Stewart's house. Scott was not present but heard an account of it afterwards from a friend. This led to a correspondence between Scott and Taylor on ballad translations. Later on Mrs Barbauld wrote to William Taylor: "Are you aware that you made Walter Scott a poet? So he told me when the other day I had the gratification of meeting him. It was, he says, your ballad of Leonora, and particularly the lines 'Tramp, tramp' &c."*

Taylor's peculiarities of language were not offensive to all. C. L. Aikin tells us that during his meridian he was constantly attended by a youthful band of admiring disciples. Nor the most familiar associate, she says, could anticipate his ready information, novel inference, strange hypothesis, ingenious illustration, ironical suggestion or playful banter, while the peculiarity of his diction, interspersed with words of his own coinage, added zest to his sayings.[2] One of Taylor's youthful protégés was Henry Southey, younger brother of the poet. He arranged for Henry to enter Michael Maurice's school at Normanston, outside Lowestoft, telling his brother that Maurice was a humane, generous, respectable man, at pains to inspire in his students habits of piety and a leaning to republican theories of government. Two years later he arranged to place Henry at Norwich under Philip Meadows Martineau the surgeon.[3]

In November 1790 William Taylor and his friend Frank Sayers were concerned in forming the Speculative Society

* The ballad is an account of her dead lover riding off with the girl Ellenore. The lines in question were:

Tramp, tramp across the land they speede:
Splash, splash, across the sea.

whose members included three Anglican clergymen, three Dissenting ministers and two doctors—Rigby and Lubbock. They met fortnightly at one another's houses. At seven precisely the chair was taken by the host, one of the members read a paper and the rest of the evening was spent in discussing it. In September 1791 Sayers read a paper entitled: "In what does beauty consist?" Beauty, he maintained, was largely determined by associations in the mind of the beholder. The society was still active in October 1797 when Dr Enfield, the Octagon minister, introduced the question: "By what means may the art of conversation be improved?" Dr Enfield died a month later and the Speculative Society did not long survive him.

Another society of literati and men of enquiring mind was the United Friars, founded in 1785 by Thomas Ransome, a clerk in Gurney's bank, noted for the beauty of his penmanship. The society intended to emulate the monks and friars in their scientific aquisitions, love of learning and philanthropy. They disclaimed everything pertaining to their religious function but would substitute decent mirth for their rules of austerity. The eight original members included William Wilkins, antiquary, architect and lessee of the Norwich theatre, William Beechey, the portrait painter, then working in Norwich, and Edward Miles a minaturist. Each member was assigned to some order of monks or friars. He was expected to equip himself with the appropriate habiliments and to read a paper on the history of his order. The society annually elected one of its members to be Abbot for the year ensuing. Others were appointed Prior, Procurator, Burser, Hospitaler, Precentor and Almoner. Among the Abbots were the Rev. John Walker, a literary parson who was also a member of the Speculative Society, Elisha De Hague, the Town Clerk, William Wilkins, Bartlett Gurney, William Stevenson, who came to the city as an artist and became proprietor of the *Norfolk Chronicle*, Edward Colman, the surgeon, and John Beckwith, the organist. They also elected as honorary members people of some distinction living out of Norwich, among them the eccentric Earl of Orford, Humphrey Repton, the landscape gardener, Sir Thomas Beevor, and Luke Hansard, the printer. Honorary members generally seem to have regarded their election as a compliment.

Many attended and were duly initiated, some corresponded and others donated books. In time the society amassed a considerable library—in 1795 they insured their effects for £100. In 1791 they moved from premises in St Martin at Palace to a house near St Andrew's Hall belonging to Henry Dobson, himself a Friar, where they rented a chapter room 27 by 20 feet and 12 feet high, a refectory 15 by 20 feet and a robing closet 6 by 14 feet, with the use of a wine-cellar for £20 a year. They met on Tuesday evenings, usually 10 or 12 of them, rarely as many as 20 being present. They interested themselves in new inventions. Henry Dobson on one occasion produced a model of a machine he had invented to convey green winter crops off wet land. Another time he read a paper on the propriety of using machines in manufactures and agriculture. Dobson was an enthusiast for French innovations. In 1792 he decided to emigrate to France and was placed on the list of honorary members. With a view to scientific experiment Bartlett Gurney presented the society with a pump and a portable chemical chest; John Harvey with an electrical machine and Thomas Suffield, the wine merchant, with a microscope. The interests of the society were wideranging. In 1792 they considered a letter from Edmund Gillingwater, the historian of Lowestoft, on means to preserve the lives of shipwrecked seamen. They later planned experiments on this project at Brother Gurney's at Wroxham. In 1796 they discussed chimney sweeping, coming to the conclusion that a less inhumane mode might be equally successful. In 1802 they considered a paper on the introduction of pure air into prisons. The slave trade was a recurrent topic. In 1795 they agreed to abstain—so far as they conveniently could—from the use of articles imported from the West Indies which appeared most likely to promote the continuance of the trade.

In January 1793, while the King was being brought to judgement in France, the society was conducting an inquiry into the situation of day husbandmen. They sent queries to a number of gentlemen in Norfolk as to day wages and additional advantages; the availability of labourers; the sufficiency of cottage accommodation; and the poor rates, comparatively for 1752, 1772 and 1792.

In its early days the society concerned itself with public

morals. Bartlett Gurney and William Wilkins were commended
for their part in suppressing the nuisance of lottery offices in
the city while the Rev. John Walker was asked to prepare for
insertion in the papers an animadversion on the abuse of the
Lord's Day by the children of the lower class of people. Later
on they devoted themselves more to science and literature.
Among subjects discussed were gravity, navigation, the solar
eclipse, the origins of alphabetic writing and the Spanish
conquest of the West Indies. They debated whether climate
had more influence on morals than government or education
and talked about the nature of genius, the determination of the
standard of taste, and the analogy between music and painting.

The United Friars were concerned to further literature and
the arts in the city. They enabled Elizabeth Bentley to publish
her *Poetical Compositions*. Elizabeth had no schooling: she was
the daughter of a journeyman cordwainer who taught her
reading and spelling and she had a natural gift for rhyming. In
1788 rejoicings in the city over a Bill in Parliament prohibiting
the exportation of wool moved her to celebrate the occasion
in verse:

> Now old Norvicum's sons once more shall hear
> The sweet harmonious sounds of joy sincere;
> Peace in her walls and commerce shall endure,
> Her Fleece protected and her trade secure.
> The city shall with all its lustre shine,
> Th' industrious indigent no more shall pine. . . .

In the next year her "poetical essays" came to the notice of
the society and in 1791 the Abbot, the Rev. John Walker—
himself an aspiring poet—and the Burser, William Stevenson,
took it upon themselves to forward her publication. They
secured upwards of 1500 subscribers, including the masters of
several Cambridge colleges and people from as far away as
Southampton, Lichfield and Sheffield. These received a slim
volume of poems with an engraving of Elizabeth Bentley's
portrait painted by another protégé of the society, Sarah Buck.
In 1790 they had presented a silver medal to Miss Buck in
return for a portrait of the Abbot which she had given to the
United Friars.

In their philanthropic activities they relieved individual cases of need, at one time allowing 6d a week to a poor Jewish woman, at another subscribing £2 2s od to the Fathers of La Trappe for the care of orphans. Every winter they collected public subscriptions and organised the distribution of soup and bread to the needy. In the winter of 1795/6, 8686 quarts of soup and penny loaves were distributed. The amount increased year by year during the lean war years until in 1800/1 no less than 38,120 portions were given out. Members were appointed weekly to satisfy themselves as to the quality of the soup supplied. Their most enduring effort resulted from John Beckwith reading a paper in 1788 on a plan for the relief of decayed tradesmen and their widows and orphans. The benevolent society formed to implement this plan has continued its work down to the present day.

Despite the fierce political antagonism of the times the United Friar's Society brought together men of both persuasions. They were even able to discuss politics on occasion though the subject was usually barred. On the day after the election of 1799 at a meeting when both whig and tory members were present their recorder entered in the book—"The conversation orange, purple and blue". In May 1799 De Hague raised the question whether the Act for the suppression of societies considered seditious and treasonable would affect their fraternity. A copy of the Act was obtained and while they were satisfied that the views entertained among them had not the most distant tendency to anything the act was framed to guard against they thought it wise to abrogate the vow binding members to secrecy concerning their affairs.

The possesion of moneyed leisure was not an absolute prerequisite for membership of the United Friars. In 1788 they decided to use their rule for admission of honorary members to admit persons resident in Norwich whose education, talents or ingenuity were likely to promote the designs of the society but whose circumstances did not permit them to subscribe. The immediate case was that of Blyth Hancock, a poor schoolmaster. During his membership he probably contributed more papers than anyone else. The calculation of the transit of Mercury, refraction of light, population, matter and motion, and the ascent of vapours were among his subjects. In 1789 he was appointed to take care of the society's philosophical and mechanical instruments, which provided an excuse for paying him 2s 6d a week. In 1791 two of the bretheren—John Harvey and Charles Marsh—obtained for him a vacancy in Doughty's Hospital. When he was ill the Brother Infirmarius was directed to visit him and he remained in membership until the Verger announced his death in June 1795.[4]

Reference has been made to several artists who were members of the United Friars. The interest in art which was to issue immediately after our period in the formation of the famous Norwich Society to inquire into "the rise, progress and present state of painting, architecture, and sculpture, with a view to point out the best methods of study and to attain to greater perfection in these arts", had been growing over the previous decade. Joseph Browne, an artist "bred up solely in the school of nature"—he had started life as a waterman—was much employed as a copier of pictures and attained a reputation as "the Norwich Claude". He lived opposite the church of St Peter Permountergate for which he painted an altar-piece of St Peter and the Cock which is still to be seen there. When he died in 1800 his "capital paintings consisting of sea and landscapes" were sold at his house.

About 1790 the two young enthusiasts John Crome and Robert Ladbrooke hired a garret together and started trying to make a living by their art. To Ladbrooke, we are told, art meant the study and imitation of the work of others; to Crome doing his own thing.[5] Somehow Crome came to the notice of Thomas Harvey of Catton and was able to study his collection of pictures including Gainsborough's Cottage Door and several of the Dutch school, and to make free of the painting room where Harvey amused himself as an amateur. It was here probably that he met Sir William Beechey and so established himself in the artist's friendship that years later when he visited London he dined and spent his evenings with him. In 1798 he was still going to Catton and there met John Opie who had recently married Amelia Alderson. Sometimes he watched Opie painting and sometimes Opie would work on Crome's canvass while the latter amused the company with droll stories and humourous observations.[6] About the same time Edmund Cotman, the haberdasher, troubled by the aspiration of his son John to be an artist, also consulted Opie, to receive the discouraging advice—"Rather let him black boots". However John Sell Cotman could not be deterred. By the end of the year he had gone to London to be an artist.[7] Three years later the United Friars elected him an honorary member of their fraternity, dispensing with the usual expenses of admission in consideration of his extraordinary talents as an artist. On the occasion of his initiation he exhibited some masterly sketches of scenes in Wales and heard the Abbot, John Beckwith, read an excellent essay comparing sacred and secular music. Cotman came home again briefly in 1802 and during his stay in the city offered to give drawing lessons at 10s 6d an hour. By this time Crome was well established as a drawing master numbering among his pupils the Gurney sisters of Earlham and earning a modest competence by his chosen profession.

An institution of learning which was generally above party politics was the Public (subscription) Library founded in 1784. Dr Enfield of the Octagon Chapel was President in 1788 followed next year by the Rev. John Pretyman, one of the Prebendaries; their politics naturally followed their religious affiliations. Another Octagon member Elias Norgate succeeded Pretyman to be followed by Dr Harrington, a Prebendary of Wells Cathedral who also held benefices in Norfolk and Suffolk. William Taylor junior, yet another Octagonian, was president in 1793. He related that when it was being considered whether to acquire a copy of the latest Constitution of France, Dr Sayers who was a member of the committee remarked, "We have just agreed not to take any more Periodical publications".[8]

The library spending £200 a year had not the means to provide a comprehensive service nor could this be expected from the booksellers though the city had about a dozen of them. So when bookish citizens travelled they were on the look-out to acquire additions for their own or their friends' shelves. W. W. Wilkin staying at Bath for his health in 1795 wrote to Joseph Kinghorn that he had found a cheap bookseller. He sent a list of likely books. He thought William Taylor might like the two quarto volumes of the *Oevres de Gravesande* and six octavos of *Philosophie de la Nature*. Would Kinghorn ask him and let Wilkin know? Later he wrote that he had sent a box of books containing "tag, rag and bobtail" by Wednesday's waggon to London. It would come on by Marsh's waggon and should arrive at Norwich the next Thursday. Marsh's waggon also brought from time to time parcels of books sent to William Taylor for review. In 1797 when Thomas Theobald, son of the breeches-maker of Cockey Lane, was in Germany on business, Kinghorn wrote to him at Leipsig asking him to get a Hebrew Bible. Thomas replied that he had obtained the Bible for 11s and that if Kinghorn wanted a hundred books he could buy them without inconvenience. This resulted in a list of German publications, six of them for William Taylor who was then teaching Kinghorn the language. Thomas arrived home in February 1798 after a rough and dangerous passage and being in imminent peril of capture by a French frigate which lost them by mere awkwardness. Kinghorn wrote, "Had Mr Theobald been taken I should have lost more than a friend for he had about 20 Vols. of books for me, all which wd have gone and it is probable I shall read them more than those who might have captured them."

Intellectual interests were not the absolute monopoly of those who had leisure and means. A case in point is that of John Fransham (1730–1810) son of the parish clerk of St George's Colegate whose education terminated at an early age owing to the death of a relation who had been prepared to pay for it. By his own efforts Fransham acquired a good deal of classical and mathematical knowledge and was able to make a living by coaching young men going to the universities or training as attorneys, chemists or doctors. He might have made a moderate income in this way but having a deep contempt for money and a principle of perfection which limited him to teaching no more than six to eight pupils at a time and a determination to be free for his studies which made him cut down his teaching to two hours a day, he earned on the average, his biographer tells us, no more than 8s a week. With this he procured the necessaries of life, incurred no debts and saved substantially to buy books. For some time, by way of experiment, he lived on ¼d worth of potatoes a day, saving one potato from each day's ration until he had an extra day's supply and could spend the ¼d saved on salt. He was a member of a society comprising men of original minds and small incomes for improvement in mathematics and experimental philosophy. Another member was Joseph Clover, a blacksmith. For a time Fransham earned a little by leading home horses after shoeing. While the iron was heating Clover and Fransham would be engaged in Latin, in which Fransham was the master, or in mathematical problems in which Clover excelled. Clover later attained some fame as a veterinary surgeon. Fransham occasionally attended meetings of the Tusculan School where he argued against the Christian faith. He believed in God as the first cause but was repelled from Christianity by the callousness of its professors in relation to animals, instancing bull and bear bating, stag and hare hunting, cock-fighting and the overburdening of horses. He was not in political sympathy with the young men of the Tusculan School, favouring absolute monarchy as likely to secure the best government. Fransham was known in Norwich for his eccentric appearance, usually wearing a short green jacket with large horn buttons, large shoes and coarse worsted stockings, and a broad hat with his long grey hair hanging about his shoulders. His writings were never published. After his death five quarto manuscript volumes of essays passed to Dr Rigby and 30 smaller manuscripts to the Stark family. His manuscripts no doubt circulated; some of those which survive in the N. & N. Record Office are not originals but copies. [9]

Few could succeed in living on so little as sufficed for John Fransham. Poor John Henry Colls who aspired to be a poet—several of his poems were read with approval to the United Friars—was eventually driven to take a commission in the 24th Regiment and to "Protract existence on an Ensign's pay". This he found inadequate and when he was dying in 1802 he directed that his poems should be published for the benefit of his wife and child. This final effort was to prove a failure—too large an edition was printed and no benefit accrued.

Another centre of learning, though somewhat detached from the city, was to be found in the Close. This was in those days a separate jurisdiction from the city, a requisite number of the Prebendaries being sworn as Justices of the Peace and an independant prison maintained. The six Prebendaries were each in residence only two months of the year. Dr Yates who was also master of St Catherine's Cambridge and in 1794 Vice Chancellor of the University no doubt spent most of his time there for he was invariably absent from meetings of the Chapter. Robert Potter, installed in 1788, whom we have met with as a patriotic preacher, received his stall as a reward for sending Lord Chancellor Thurlow a copy of his translation of Sophocles. Even the Dean was often absent. Philip Lloyd wrote from Naples in 1788 giving the Chapter authority to seal various leases and Joseph Turner, who succeeded him in 1790, often gave similar instructions, writing sometimes from Bath and sometimes from Cambridge. All this no doubt lent colour to Richard Dinmore's complaint of lazy deans and idle prebendaries. Yet some of the prebendaries did participate in the life of the city. Dr John Pretyman, though he held simultaneously a stall at Lincoln cathedral, was as we have seen president of the library and he also sometimes took the chair at the Board meetings of the hospital. The Close had an appeal to men of literary aspirations which occasioned Dr Frank Sayers settling there in 1792. As his friend William Taylor wrote, the classical acquirements, the gentlemanly manners, the respectable morality, the liberal leisure, so general among the English clergy, fitted them for his companions and they became his favourite society. As a youth Sayers studied medicine at Edinburgh and in London. He went to Leyden to graduate but ultimately received his M.D. from Hardervyke "a less celebrated and less scrupulous university". As he never intended to practice medicine perhaps this did not matter. Brought up at the Octagon he was accustomed to worship there till his mother's death in 1790. He later became a frequenter of Cathedral worship, "which from the imposing majesty of its theatre and its execution" appealed to his serious and profound piety. He wrote his Disquisitions, first published in 1793, and a number of poems, he studied Greek, he kept a horse and gig to amuse himself with pilgrimages to churches within a day's drive, and he delighted to exercise his conversational powers, becoming, Taylor says, the first man in Norwich to whom a stranger would covet to be introduced.[10] He was happiest

in the meetings of small convivial clubs. He wrote for one
such:

> Dinners of form I vote a bore,
> Where folks who never met before
> And care not if they ne'er meet more
> Are brought together.
> Crammed close as mackerel in their places
> They eat with Chesterfieldian graces,
> Drink healths and talk with sapient faces
> About the weather.
> Thrice blest who at an inn unbends
> With half a dozen of his friends
> . . . . ; . . .[11]

When Sayers formed an intention of leaving his library to the
Dean and Chapter he burned what he considered heretical—
the works of Voltaire and Hume and one of William Taylor's
pamphlets of Biblical Criticism. The Chapter ultimately received some 600 books under his will.[12]

In music the Close led the city. The veteran Cathedral
organist, Thomas Garland, appointed in 1749 at the age of 18,
was wont to arrange concerts at the Assembly House and
elsewhere. A school for choristers was maintained—in 1794
the master's salary was increased from £16 to £20 a year in
consideration of his teaching the boys arithmatic as well as
reading and writing.[13] Annual oratorios were performed for
the benefit of the hospital when choristers from the Octagon,
which also trained a number of singing boys, were customarily
brought in to share the work with the choir of the Cathedral.[14]
If the Close with its strong tendency to be conservative influenced the city, it was inevitable that the city should also
influence the Close. The two daughters of Prebendary Robert
Plumptre became enthusiastic "jacobins"—perhaps it was as
well that their father did not live to see it; he died in 1788.
Annabella Plumptre was a contributor to *The Cabinet* while her
sister Anne, who was something of an authoress, wrote in 1795
to her literary agent in London addressing him as "Dear
Citizen" and expressing her admiration of John Thelwall.[15]

A not unimportant contributor to the cultural life of the city

was Doctor, afterwards Sir, James Edward Smith, son of a
Norwich merchant. After studying at Edinburgh and obtaining
a medical degree at Leyden, Smith went to London and devoted
himself to the study of botany. He was befriended by Sir
Joseph Banks the president of the Royal Society. After the
death of the Swedish scientist, Carl Linnaeus, the father of
systematic botany, Banks was offered his library and natural
history collection. Not wishing to take up the offer himself he
passed it on to J. E. Smith who purchased the collection with
help from his father. In 1788 Smith became the first president
of the Linnaean Society which was formed at a meeting in his
house in Great Marlborough St, London. He was in Norwich
in the summer of 1794 when he gave a course of eighteen
lectures on zoology and botany at a charge of £2 2s 0d. Two
years later he married and much against the advice of his
friends settled in Norwich. The Bishop of Carlisle wrote to
him:

> At the distance of Norwich you will be quite buried
> alive. . . . How necessary it is "that he who would reign
> over many must be perpetually contending with many" . . .
> You will have nobody to question your authority in
> Norwich.[16]

Yet he came and settled down in Norwich, spending part of
each spring in London. In 1799 William Taylor entrusted him
with a letter to Southey, writing: "You will have a satisfaction
in making the acquaintance not merely of the first botanist in
Europe . . . but of a man whose aimiable temper and excellance
of heart are worthy to be known by you."[17]

Besides his scientific activities J. E. Smith became a deacon
of the Octagon congregation for which he wrote a number of
hymns.

William Taylor tried to enrich the literary society of Norwich
by persuading Robert Southey to settle here, urging that house-
rent was very cheap and society as agreeable as in most places.
Southey replied that the letter excited a half desire to diet for
life upon Norfolk puddings, turnips and turkeys if destiny did
not invite to a better city. He was just then hoping to go to
Italy as secretary to the legation. Taylor did not himself take

an unduly rosy view of Norwich society. "Contented medi-
ocrity", he wrote, "is always the ultimate destiny of us pro-
vincials."[18]

REFERENCES

 1. J. W. Robberds, *Life of Wm. Taylor*, vol. I, p. 43.
 2. J. W. Robberds, op. cit., vol. I, p. 570.
 3. J. W. Robberds, op. cit., vol. I, pp. 234, 365.
 4. *Transactions of the United Friars Society*, N. & N. Record Office.
 5. S. C. Kaines Smith, *Crome*, p. 22.
 6. S. C. Kaines Smith, *Crome*, p. 33.
 7. S. D. Kitson, *Life of John Sell Cotman*, p. 9.
 8. W. Taylor, *Collective Works of the late Dr Sayers*, LXXVI.
 9. W. Saint, *Memoirs of the late John Fransham*.
10. W. Taylor, op. cit., LXXVI.
11. J. W. Robberds, op. cit., vol. I, p. 42.
12. J. W. Robberds, op. cit., vol. I, p. 476.
13. Norwich Cathedral Chapter Book.
14. John Taylor, *History of the Octagon Chapel*, p. 59.
15. Plumptre MSS, N. & N. Record Office.
16. Lady Smith, *Memoir of the late Sir J. E. Smith*, p. 527.
17. J. W. Robberds, op. cit., vol. I, p. 270.
18. J. W. Robberds, op. cit., vol. I, p. 355.

APPENDIX A MANUSCRIPT SOURCES

NRO = Norfolk and Norwich Record Office
PRO = Public Record Office, London

Bell Corporation Club Minute Book	NRO
Chapter Books, Norwich Cathedral Library	
Churchwardens' Accounts of Norwich Parishes	NRO
J. Cozens, Account Books	NRO
John DeCarle and Philip Barnes, Document	NRO
John Fransham, Political Tracts	NRO
Friendly Societies, Articles of Association	NRO
Gurney MSS, Friends' House Library, London	
Elizabeth Gurney's Journal, Friends' House Library, London	
Gurney's Bank Ledgers, Barclay's Bank Ltd, London	
Home Office Papers re Volunteers (HO/50)	PRO
Kinghorn's Papers, in possession of the author	
London Corresponding Society Papers, British Museum. Adds. MSS. 27811, 27812.	
Col. J. Money, Letters to the Lord Lieutenant	NRO
Norfolk and Norwich Hospital, Committee Books, Hospital Archives	
Norwich Corporation Assembly Books	NRO
Norwich Guardians of the Poor Minute Books	NRO
Norwich Court of Mayoralty Books	NRO
Norwich Hospitals Committee Books	NRO
Norwich Public Library Committee Minutes. Norfolk & Norwich Library	
Norwich Quarter Sessions Books	NRO
Norwich Roll of Freemen	NRO
Norwich Sacramental Certificates	NRO
Augustine Noverre, House Expenses Book	NRO
A. Plumptre, Letters	NRO
Privy Council Papers re Corresponding Societies	PRO
Richard Reece's Diary, Wesley's Chapel, London	
Treasury Solicitor's Papers (TS 24)	PRO

Tusculanum (Minutes of the Tusculan School)   NRO
Transactions of the Society of United Friars   NRO
Visitation Papers, 1801   NRO
Wilkin Papers   NRO
John Woodrow's Cash Journal   NRO

APPENDIX B PRINTED CONTEMPORARY OR NEAR-CONTEMPORARY SOURCES

Thomas Amyot, *Speeches in Parliament of William Windham*, London, 1812

Annual Registers

Joel Barlow, *Advice to the Privileged Orders*, London, 1793

R. Beatniffe, *Norfolk Tour*, Norwich, 1795

E. Bentley, *Poetical Compositions*, Norwich, 1791

Samuel Breame, *Essay to Investigate the Expenditure on Account of the Poor*, Norwich, ND

S. W. Browne and J. Darken, *Address of the Patriotic Society of Norwich*, Norwich, 1797

W. Earle Bulwer, *Standing Orders of the Norwich or 106th Regiment*, Waterford, 1795

The Cabinet, By a Society of Gentlemen, Norwich, 1795

W. Chase, *The Norwich Directory*, Norwich, 1783

J. H. Colls, *Poems*, Norwich, c.1803

Richard Dinmore jnr, *Exposition of the Principles of the English Jacobins*, Norwich, 1797

William Enfield, *A Selection of Hymns for Social Worship*, Norwich, 1795

William Firth, *An Address to the Electors of Norwich*, Norwich, 1794

Samuel Fisher, *Consistency the Test of Truth*, Norwich, 1795

A. Geddes, *A Norfolk Tale*, London, 1792

P. Gedge, *Impartial Account of the Dispute between Sir Thomas Beevor, Bart., and John Money Esq.*, Bury, 1788

William Godwin, *Enquiry concerning Political Justice*, London, 1796

Charles Harvey, *Charge to the Grand Jury of the City and County of Norwich*, Norwich, 1793

Joshua Larwood, *Erratics by a Sailor*, London, 1800

W. Lorkin, *First Establishment of Wesleyan Methodism in Norwich*, Norwich, 1825

James Mackintosh, *Vindiciae Gallicae*, London, 1791

J. March, *Proceedings and Speeches at the Meeting on 17th Nov. 1795 at St Andrew's Hall Norwich to petition Parliament against Lord Grenville's and Mr Pitt's Treason and Sedition Bills*, Norwich, 1795

Jonathon Matchett, *Norfolk and Norwich Remembrancer*, Norwich, 1822

T. Mendham, *Rights of Man*, Norwich, 1791

J. Money, *History of the Campaign of 1792 between the armies of France and the Allies*, London, 1794

Norfolk and Norwich Parliamentary Addresses, Norwich, 1768–1830

The Norfolk Chronicle or Norwich Gazette, 1788–1802

The Norwich Mercury, 1788–1802

Norwich, Address to the Electors, Norwich, 1794

Norwich, Election Budget, Norwich, 1796

Norwich, Evidence on the petition by which the election of H. Hobart was declared void, Norwich, 1787

Norwich, New Election Budget, Norwich, 1786

Norwich, One of the People. A Letter to the Society which met at the Angel to celebrate the birthday of C. J. Fox, Norwich, 1799

Norwich, Political Pamphlets, Norwich, 1734–1823

Norwich, Poll Books, Parliamentary Elections, Norwich, 1786, 1787, 1790, 1794, 1796, 1799, & 1802

Norwich, Poll Book, Sheriff's election, Norwich, 1796

Thomas Peck, *The Norwich Directory*, Norwich, 1802

R. Potter, *Sermon before the Mayor and Corporation*, Norwich, 1793

R. Potter, *Sermon for the 1st June 1802*, Norwich, 1802

W. Richards, *Reflections on French Atheism*, Lynn, 1794

E. Rigby, *Reports of the Special Provision Committee appointed by the Court of Guardians of the city of Norwich*, London, 1788

J. G. Robberds, *Sermons by the late Rev. Pendlebury Houghton*, London, 1825

W. Saint, *Memoirs of the late John Fransham of Norwich*, Norwich, 1811

J. Sillett, *Views of the Churches, Chapels and Public Edifices in the City of Norwich*, Norwich, 1828
J. E. Smith, *Biographical Memoirs of several Norwich Botanists*, Norwich, 1804
State Trials, Complete Collection of, vols XXIV and XXV
W. Taylor, *Collective Works of the late Dr Sayers*, Norwich, 1823
J. Thellwall, *The late attrocious Proceedings at Yarmouth*, London, 1796
John Wesley, The Journal of, vol. IV, London, 1827
Sarah Wilks, *Memoir of the Rev. Mark Wilks*, London, 1821
Mark Wilks, *Two Sermons on the Origin and Stability of the French Revolution*, Norwich, 1791
Mark Wilks, *Athaliah. Two Collection Sermons*, Norwich, 1795
William Winterbotham, *The Trial of, at Exeter, 1793*, London, 1794

APPENDIX C BOOKS

Mme. D'Arblay, *Diary and Letters*, London, 1891
Bacon and Kinnebrook, *Memoir of the late P. M. Martineau*, Norwich, 1831
Mrs Henry Baring, *Diary of the Rt. Hon. Wm. Windham*, London, 1866
Sir Francis Bateman and Walter Rye, *History of the Bethel Hospital*, Norwich, 1906
A. Batty-Shaw, *N. & N. Hospital. Lives of the Medical Staff*, Barford, 1971
A. D. Bayne, *Comprehensive history of Norwich*, Norwich, 1859
E. T. Blakely, *History of Norwich Manufactures*, Norwich, ND
George Borrow, *Lavengro* (Everyman Edition), London, 1924
C. L. Brightwell, *Memorials of the Life of Amelia Opie*, Norwich, 1854
John Browne, *History of Congregationalism in Norfolk and Suffolk*, London, 1877
Edmund Burke, *Reflections on the Revolution in France* (Everyman edition), London
Lord Cockburn, *Life of Lord Jeffrey*, Edinburgh, 1852

M. D. Conway, *Writings of Thomas Paine*, New York and London, 1894

Copemans of Norwich 1789–1946, Norwich, 1946

B. Cozens-Hardy and E. A. Kent, *Mayors of Norwich*, Norwich, 1938

B. Cozens-Hardy, *Mary Hardy's Diary*, Norwich, 1968

R. W. Davis, *Dissent in Politics. 1780–1830. Life of Wm. Smith MP*, London, 1971

Edward Deacon, *Samuel Fisher, Baptist Minister*, Bridgeport, U.S.A., 1911

Wm. Frederick Dickes, *The Norwich School of Painting*, London and Norwich, 1905

Dictionary of National Biography (cited as DNB)

Sir Peter Eade, *The Norfolk and Norwich Hospital 1770–1900*, London, 1900

Sir Peter Eade, *The Parish of St Giles, Norwich,* London and Norwich, 1906

Lady Eastlake, *Dr Rigby's Letters from France in 1789*, London, 1880

John Hookham Frere, *Works*, London, 1872

J. J. Gurney, *Memoirs*, Norwich, 1855

J. L. and B. Hammond, *The Skilled Labourer 1760–1832*, London, 1919

J. L. and B. Hammond, *The Town Labourer 1760–1832*, London, 1928

A. J. C. Hare, *The Gurneys of Earlham*, London, 1895

Cyril Jolly, *The Spreading Flame (Methodism in Norfolk)*, ND

R. W. Ketton-Cremer, *The early Life & Diaries of Wm. Windham*, London, 1930

R. W. Ketton-Cremer, *Forty Norfolk Essays*, Norwich, 1961

S. D. Kitson, *Life of John Sell Cotman*, London, 1937

R. J. Mackintosh, *Memoir of the Life of Sir James Mackintosh*, London, 1835

R. H. Mason, *History of Norfolk*, London, Part III, 1883; Part IV, 1884

H. W. Meikle, *Scotland and the French Revolution*, Glasgow, 1912

W. A. Money, *Crown Point*, Norwich, ND

R. H. Mottram, *John Crome of Norwich*, London, 1931

R. H. Mottram, *Success to the Mayor*, London, 1937

Frank Newman, *Two Centuries of Mancroft Music*, Lowestoft, 1932

A. J. Nixeaman, *The Intwood Story*, Norwich, 1972

William Cobbett, *Parliamentary History of England*, London, 1816

J. W. Robberds, *Life and Writings of the late Wm. Taylor of Norwich*, London, 1843

W. Roberts, *Sir William Beechey*, London, 1907

Betsy Rodgers, *Georgian Chronicle* (re Mrs Barbauld), London, 1958

Janet Ross, *Three Generations of Englishwomen*, London, 1888

Walter Rye, *Norfolk Families*, Norwich, 1913

H. W. Saunders, *History of Norwich Grammar School*, Norwich, 1932

S. C. Kaines Smith, *John Crome*, London, 1923

Lady Smith, *Memoir and Correspondence of the late Sir James Edward Smith*, London, 1832

John Stacey, *General History of the County of Norfolk*, Norwich, 1829

John Taylor and Edward Taylor, *History of the Octagon Chapel, Norwich*, London, 1848

John Taylor, *Hymns and miscellaneous Poems*, London, 1863

E. P. Thompson, *The Making of the English Working Class* (Pelican Edition), London, 1970

Mary Thrale, *Autobiography of Francis Place (1771–1854)*, Cambridge, 1972

E. A. Tillett, *The Tokens of Norfolk*, Norwich, 1882

Dawson Turner, *Etchings of the late John Crome with a Biographical Memoir*, Norwich, ND

J. Steven Watson, *The Reign of George III 1760–1815*, Oxford, 1960

M. H. Wilkin, *Joseph Kinghorn of Norwich*, Norwich, 1855

James Woodforde, *Diary of a Country Parson*, Oxford, 1968

INDEX

Index

M